When God Chose a Father

Discovering God's Desire to Be Intimately Involved In Your Life

Michael F. Clark

ISBN:978-1-7370596-0-8
Copyright © 2021 by Michael F. Clark
Michael Clark Ministries
P.O. Box 3131
Broken Arrow, OK 74013
www.michaelclarkministries.org

ACKNOWLEDGEMENTS

I would like to extend a big "Thank You" to the following people who have helped me make "When God Chose a Father" a reality. Their encouragement, advice, and expertise have been invaluable.

Editorial Consultant and Constant Encourager –
Andrell Corbin

Proofing and Feedback –
Susan Woodrow
Veronica Bagby

Manuscript Editor – Marilyn Price

Typesetting – Lisa Simpson, Simpson Productions

Cover Art – Debbie Pullman,
Zoe Life Creative Media

Ed McConnell Design

TABLE OF CONTENTS

FOREWORD

Writing *When God Chose a Father* has been a journey, as the concept grew over years of raising my children and navigating the twists and turns of life. I laid down the book for a period of time while I battled cancer, but eventually picked it up again and finished what was in my heart to write.

As I looked on my life, I was overcome with how personal God had been in situation after situation of my life. He was always there, watching over me, ready to help me make it through each day. I realized that the care and support I enjoyed came from a loving father and mother, a wonderful wife, and four children—all who loved me even when I wasn't that loveable. They each are a gift from God, and my hope is that in the following pages I can effectively share some of the lessons I have learned that have made my life have purpose. Your life has purpose as well, and God wants to help you both see your purpose and accomplish it.

I'd like to thank my wife, Rebecca, for being my best friend and walking through life with me. We've been doing the parent thing for many years now, and there's no one I'd rather be pursuing God's plan with than you.

To my children, thank you for loving me and allowing me to be "Dad," jokes and all. I love each of you with all that I am, and have learned so much from you. To my firstborn, Tony, I again apologize for having little clue of what I was doing when we started out together. Your sisters benefited from the learning experiences I had with you.

Lastly, I want to thank my dad, Emory, for being such a wonderful model of a father. In these pages I discuss several aspects of who you are to me and have meant to me. I can look at God as my loving Heavenly Father because of the loving earthly father I had in you, You will always be my hero, and I love you more than I can express.

INTRODUCTION

"Jesus loves me, this I know. For the Bible tells me so."

I learned this at an early age, even before I could read. My parents took me to church every Sunday, but it wasn't only there that I heard those words. My parents shared them with me at home and showed me by their lives. It helped form a foundation for me to believe that God was interested in me and my life.

Years later I became a father, and the new dimension of parenthood showed me that I didn't have all the answers for raising a child. I had been around kids my whole life, but the responsibility of being a parent was new. I loved my little boy, and realized that everything I was going to do with him was going to have an impact on him and his future. I didn't want to screw things up.

I had lost my mom in a car wreck when I was twelve. With her gone, my dad had to raise a teenaged boy alone. He was strong, yet patient. He had high expectations, but was kind. He had always been my hero. My mom and I had been close, and it was hard to have her disappear from my life in one icy afternoon. Dad did the best he could and helped to remind me in the hard times that God loved me and I wasn't alone.

It was trust in God that got me through my teen years. It was that same trust that had me sitting in my bedroom one night thinking about raising my little boy and how best to do it. My father had been a wonderful role model, and he had worked to instill values in me that were based on God's Word. As I pondered on how I was to be that role model to my son, I knew I needed guidance. I turned to God for help and answers.

Now that little boy has become a man and made me a grandfather. As I watch him with his little boy, I think back to those days when I was in his shoes. So much love and enjoyment, and so much responsibility. I am so thankful that I learned that Jesus loves me and that God had a plan. Being a parent is a great responsibility, but we were never intended to wander in the dark, feeling alone with no guiding light. God has a plan for every child and for every parent of a child. He wants the best for all involved.

I was never alone in life, because God wanted to be a part of it. He wasn't picking and choosing which days He preferred to be involved in—He wanted to be involved in every single one. I came to understand that as involved as I wanted to be in every single day of my little boy's life, God wanted the same level of involvement in mine.

Watching my son with his little boy, I'm reminded of why I wrote *When God Chose a Father*. All those years ago when I asked God for help in learning to be the father He wanted me to be to my son, He gave me homework. I was told to study the life of Joseph, the man He chose to be the earthly father of His Son. My studies showed me the characteristics God wanted me to develop to be a good parent. I was to do my best to model the character and values of God to my children. That was God's intention with Joseph, and it's the same with you and me. My studies also showed me how involved God wanted to be in our lives and the love He has for us. Just as I worked to pass those things along to my son, I want to share them with you as well.

You and I are not alone. God is willing and ready to be as much a part of our lives as we'll allow Him to be. Nothing is too small or too large. He gave a part of Himself in the form of a newborn baby in order to bring us back into relationship with Him. He chose the parents for that child, and then moved in their lives to help them be the parents He had called them to be. He chose parents who would listen to His voice and seek after Him with their hearts. Those are both things that you and I can do. When we do those things, we can look to Him to be with us and help us. We see this principle in the book of Jeremiah where the prophet Jeremiah spoke to the Israelites who had been in exile for 70 years, giving them the following promise from God:

Jeremiah 29:11-13:

> *For I know the thoughts that I think toward you, says the Lord. They are thoughts of peace and not of evil, to give you a future and a hope.*
>
> *Then you will call upon Me and go and pray to Me, and I will listen to you.*

You will seek Me and find Me, when you search for Me with all your heart.

God's always has thoughts and plans and a future and a hope for those who love Him. He wants to be intimately involved in your life to help you have hope and to see you obtain that future He has ordained for you. What He needs from you is to be an *active participant* in the plan He has for you and for each of us. It will require you to seek Him, hear from Him, and act on what you hear. In the coming pages you will see how God chose a man in Joseph who followed this pattern to fulfill the role God had chosen for him. You have a role that you were chosen for as well.

The good news is, God isn't leaving you empty-handed. He will be with you every step of the way and has given you grace to do all that He will ask of you.

Years ago when I was going through a difficult time I came across the following verse: *"Let your conduct be without covetousness* [love of money]*; be content with such things as you have. For He Himself has said: 'I will never leave you nor forsake you'"* (Hebrews 13:5).

I read it over several times, and while it was comforting to me, it really didn't register deep inside me until I heard it this way: *"I will never leave your side, and I will never leave you hung out to dry."*

While it sounded more like the playground translation, I finally got the point. If I stuck close to God, He would never leave me *"hung out to dry."* People can stay beside you, but hold back in their defending or aiding you. That leaves you *"hung out to dry."* What God is saying is that He has your back. Seek Him and follow after Him. Whether it is raising kids, doing business, etc., look to do things His way.

As you will see in Joseph's life, God's way is not always the easy way—but it is the way to a future and a hope. Learning about Joseph helped me to see the character traits that God wanted to grow in me and to pass on to others. When we honor the things of God, He will honor us.

It is my hope that as you read this book you will find answers that you have been searching for, and that they will lead you further down the road of being all that God has created you to be.

God chose Joseph for a reason, and He's chosen you for a reason as well.

Blessings,

Mike

Chapter 1

〰

WHAT IF YOU COULD CHOOSE THE PERSON TO RAISE YOUR CHILD?

What if you were given the chance to choose the person who was to raise your child? For whatever reason, you were not going to be in the picture, yet you were going to be able to choose a person to represent you in your child's life. From that person's birth to the day your child was placed in this person's care, you were fully informed and keenly aware of all there was to know about them. You were allowed to watch their actions, observe their attitudes—even know their most intimate details. No stone would be left unturned; there would be no unknown skeleton lurking in a closet—you would know *everything*.

You could scour a list of thousands upon thousands of eligible people in search for that person who best exemplified what you wanted to be modeled before your child, and who would best give all that you desire for your child to have in a parent. This person would do their best to be everything you wanted to have been to your child on a daily basis. You would realize that this person won't meet every qualification in full because they are, after all, human. Knowing this, you would choose the one who came the closest to what you desire, in spite of their frailties.

In reality, people rarely get a chance to know who might replace them, and the option to know everything about that replacement and handpick them is unheard of. It just doesn't happen. Life happens in real time, with little to no warning. I realized this firsthand in my own life when my mother was killed in a car wreck when I was twelve years old. She was on her way to work one winter afternoon when her car left the slick roadway, sending it airborne. It eventually hit a culvert and ended her life on impact. I was the youngest of five children and the only one still at home. One minute she was driving along to work, the next minute she was no longer physically in my life. All the things she had planned on telling me, teaching me, and experiencing with me were no longer an option. She didn't get a chance to think about who would take her place in my life or the lives of my other family members. There were no final notes, and no last minute good-byes. She was gone.

Tragic scenarios like this happen every day, impacting lives in ways that were never expected. Those whom we love are taken with no advance notice, gone with no preparation.

That loved one who is suddenly gone didn't have the chance to contemplate what void they would be leaving in others' lives and who would be best suited to fill that void in their absence. I'm sure my mom would have liked to have had the opportunity to review and select the person who could represent her in my life once she was gone. She would know what she had planned to impart to me and how she wanted to love me as I grew. I'm sure there was much she had planned for her future with me, and then in a moment she was no longer going to be able to do any of those things.

This brings us back to the original question: "What if you were given the chance to choose the person who was to raise your child?" What if you knew you weren't going to be there physically to be the mom or dad they needed?

Finding the Best Representative

If I had this chance, you can be assured I would be meticulous in my research to find the person who would be the best influence and example I wanted for my child. My children are very precious to me. I can't envision not being in their lives. They bring me so much warmth, joy, and fulfillment. A simple "I love you, Daddy" rings in my heart and never grows old. I would think long and hard about what they need to be happy, grow up in wisdom, and feel fulfilled. Then I would do my very best to find that one special person who would best represent what I hold near and dear to me and impart it to them.

17

I would want someone who loves them as much as I do. This special person would be someone who would teach them, be patient, kind, and gentle when he dealt with them. I would want someone who would look at my child as if he was of his own flesh and blood. I would look for a person who would raise them in a home full of compassion, respect, and honor. I would want that person to be an example to them of what a good man would be, a man who lived what he taught and who had a genuine regard for those around him. I would seek a man who was able to say "I'm Sorry"; a man who was strong but humble; a man who saw the good and potential in others and encouraged my child to be all God had created him to be. I'm sure I would want that man to be more than what either he or I was capable of truly being, but I would want him to do all he could to be as close as possible.

Knowing how much I love my children and the lengths I would go to if I was able to research and choose a father for them, I would venture to say that you probably feel much the same if you were the one having to make the choice for your own child. Now think of God Almighty preparing to send His only Son to earth in human form. This Son will have emptied Himself of His divine power in order to function in the world as a man. While divine in nature, His life would be lived among men as one of them, facing the same temptations and limitations, yet overcoming them as a servant of the living God empowered by His Holy Spirit. In doing this He would fulfill what man could not, and in giving His life freely, He could restore what man was incapable of restoring on his own.

What Does God Look for in Those He Chooses?

With this in mind, I believe we need to examine how God went about choosing whom He would use. There are many examples in the Bible of men and women that God has used to perform His will. Some are more exemplary people than others, as we see in leaders such as Samson who brought reproach upon himself by how he conducted himself. God uses imperfect people all of the time. Their bad choices don't negate what He saw in them; their choices only serve to reveal their level of dedication to be that person He saw in them.

There were those who were chosen to deliver God's people from bondage, fighting those who oppressed the children of Israel. Others were chosen to lead that same nation of Israel and were given the unique responsibility of serving as God's representative. What we can see is that God's method of choosing people is much different than what we see in the world, either in times of old or today. The best example is described in 1 Samuel, chapter 16.

God sent the prophet Samuel to visit Jesse the Bethlehemite to anoint the next king of Israel. Samuel systematically went through Jesse's sons looking for the young man that God had chosen:

First Samuel 16:6-13 states:

So it was, when they came, that he looked at Eliab and said, "Surely the Lord's anointed is before Him!"

But the Lord said to Samuel, **"Do not look at his appearance or at his physical stature, because I have refused him. For the Lord does not see as man sees; for man looks at the outward appearance, but the Lord looks at the heart.**" (Emphasis in this verse is mine.)

So Jesse called Abinadab, and made him pass before Samuel. And he said, "Neither has the Lord chosen this one."

Then Jesse made Shammah pass by. And he said, "Neither has the Lord chosen this one."

Thus Jesse made seven of his sons pass before Samuel. And Samuel said to Jesse, "The Lord has not chosen these."

And Samuel said to Jesse, "Are all the young men here?" Then he said, "There remains yet the youngest, and there he is, keeping the sheep." And Samuel said to Jesse, "Send and bring him. For we will not sit down till he comes here."

So he sent and brought him in. Now he was ruddy, with bright eyes, and good-looking. And the Lord said, "Arise, anoint him; for this is the one!"

Then Samuel took the horn of oil and anointed him in the midst of his brothers; and the Spirit of the Lord came upon David from that day forward. So Samuel arose and went to Ramah.

Notice that God looked at the heart of each of Jesse's sons to find the man He would choose to lead His people. This

David, Jesse's youngest son, was the same man that later God would say of him: *"The Lord has sought for Himself a man after His own heart, and the Lord has commanded him to be commander over His people . . ."* (1 Samuel 13:14).

In Acts, chapter 13, we also find Paul speaking the following of David:

> *"He raised up for them David as king, to whom also He gave testimony and said, 'I have found David the son of Jesse, a man after My own heart, who will do all My will'"* (v. 22).

When God looked at David, He looked into his heart to see inside his motivations and his attitudes. He looked to see what David had reverence for and what David's level of faithfulness was to obey Him. He looked for someone who sought to know Him, who trusted Him, and who endeavored to live a life pleasing to Him in both attitude and action.

When God looked at David,
He looked into his heart to see inside
his motivations and his attitudes.

Did David have his failings? Yes, they're described in the Old Testament in the books of 2 Samuel and 1 Chronicles. But David's heart was always intent to repent for his sins and seek to have his fellowship with God restored. God knew that David would make mistakes, as he was an imperfect man.

Every man God had to choose from was imperfect. In that knowledge He also saw a man who truly wanted to do what was right in God's eyes and was quick to correct himself when he realized that he had done something that wasn't up to God's standards.

In contrast, Saul had been chosen by the people of Israel to be their king according to their standards. God had allowed them their choice and later showed regret for doing so, as Saul faltered and failed as king. (See 1 Samuel 15:11.) God then made His own choice for Israel's king, using His standards. This is important because just as God used His standards to choose the man to be the king over the nation of Israel that was so precious to Him, He also chose the man to be the earthly parent for His precious Son.

Just as you or I would painstakingly search for the right parents for our precious child, God did the same. In Luke 11:11-13 we find that God isn't overseeing this all from some distant vantage point in the heavens. He is paying close attention:

> *If a son asks for bread from any father among you, will he give him a stone? Or if he asks for a fish, will he give him a serpent instead of a fish?*
>
> *Or if he asks for an egg, will he offer him a scorpion?*
>
> *If you then, being evil, know how to give good gifts to your children, how much more will your heavenly Father give the Holy Spirit to those who ask Him!*

Matthew 10:29-31 states:

Are not two sparrows sold for a copper coin? And not one of them falls to the ground apart from your Father's will.

But the very hairs of your head are all numbered.

Do not fear therefore; you are of more value than many sparrows.

God Pays Specific Attention to You and to Me

God's attention to you and me is at a very direct level. He knows the number of hairs on your head and mine. Think about that for a moment. That is an amazing statement. With over six billion people on this planet, God knows how many hairs are on each head. He remembers how many hairs were on the bald head before they all disappeared! That's some attention to detail!

Not only that, but He desires to give good gifts to His children. It's not enough to hand them something to hush them up—He prefers *good gifts*. Later in chapter 7 we'll look into this attention at a deeper level. At this point it suffices to say that God desires to be intimately involved in our lives, and in the life of His own Son He was very deliberate.

With this attention to detail, His search for an earthly father for His Son definitely would have been a thorough search. There would have been any number of men and women whom you or I would have looked at from the socially acceptable strata of society —well connected, well liked, and expertly instructed. The cream of Jewish society would have been candidates in our eyes. God looked at them all, and then looked outside of the criteria man would have deemed necessary. Just as He did with David, He chose those parents by what was in their hearts. He found a young maiden whose heart was inclined to Him, one who was willing to say, "*Let it be to me according to your word,.*" even though doing so would put her at odds with all those she loved and would put her very life in jeopardy. In the same manner He would have looked for and selected a man whose heart was inclined to Him, one who would obey the instructions he was given faithfully even if doing so would cause him possible hardship and reproach.

Knowing what would be required of His Son, God would choose a man whose obedience was resolute through both good times and not so good times. *How* this man would handle those times was just as important as the fact that he did handle them. Things had to be handled in a way pleasing to the Father. This man would be a living, breathing representative of God Almighty to His Son.

I'd feel the same way, and I would venture to say you would, too. It wouldn't be enough that the man I was reviewing provided for my child. I'd want him to do it with his eye always on the reason he was doing it. The trust expressed in what he was asked to do should have value to him.

WHAT IF YOU COULD CHOOSE THE PERSON TO RAISE YOUR CHILD?

I have to admit that over the years there have been days at work where the events of the workday really didn't cause me to see things as a privilege. It was when I got home to those little ones who had been waiting all day to see me, the griping customers and misguided boss all faded away, and I remembered why I put up with it. It was that beautiful woman who was looking at me in relief that I was finally home to help. It was those little faces who were so excited to see Daddy, even if I smelled like lettuce from the produce section I had stocked before I headed home. They were my reason.

They weren't my burden. I put my hand to what I could so that I could provide for the treasures God had placed in my life.

I'd want the man who took my place as my representative to look at my child like that. Even though my child wasn't his biologically, I'd want him to feel that way about him. As he looked on my child's face, he would see it as an honor to serve as Dad, just as it is mine to be Dad to my children. The honor wouldn't be rooted only in who he was representing, but also in who he was chosen to become to the child.

What's Done When No One Is Looking Counts

Selecting this person would be a meticulous process. When I looked at the example of how David was chosen to be the next king of Israel, I saw a few things that went beyond the surface. So often I had looked at the story of David as it moved forward in the Bible, weaving through the books of

1 and 2 Samuel. What I found is that this was David's story *after* he had been chosen. What led to him being chosen was greatly influenced by how he had been living his life *before* he was chosen.

As the youngest of Jesse's sons, David would have held a lesser place in the family pecking order. His inheritance would have been a lesser portion than his eldest brother's. He had not lived as long a life as his brothers, nor had their experiences, or been exposed to outside opportunities as his older brothers had been. Yet it was this youngest son of Jesse who not only caught God's eye, but won over His heart and caused Him to choose this teen boy over every other man in Israel to become God's appointed leader of His nation.

King Saul had fallen from his position because of his actions during and after his battle with the Amalekites, the account of which can be found in 1 Samuel 15. God had pronounced judgment on the Amalekites for their previous treatment of the Israelites and had instructed King Saul to attack the Amalekites and destroy them, sparing nothing—no person, no livestock. King Saul gathered his forces and attacked the Amalekites, winning a great victory. Yet King Saul did not do as God had instructed and spared the Amalekite king and the best of the flocks. To this point, God tells Samuel the following in 1 Samuel 15:10-11 NLT:

> *Then the Lord said to Samuel,*
>
> *"I am sorry that I ever made Saul king, for he has not been loyal to me and has refused to obey my command." . . .*

God passed judgment over Saul because Saul had proven to God that he was not loyal to Him and had not obeyed His command. Saul allowed himself to believe his position gave him the right to handle things as he desired, even if that went against what God had instructed. In reading the full account of Saul, you will see a man whose loyalty had become to himself and his throne and not first and foremost to God. That eventually led him to be disobedient to God's instructions, as he took liberties with his interpretation of what God had commanded him.

As we read in 1 Samuel 16:1 NLT, Samuel is still mourning King Saul's failure to please God and his pending removal from the throne of Israel:

> *Now the Lord said to Samuel, "You have mourned long enough for Saul. I have rejected him as king of Israel, so fill your flask with olive oil and go to Bethlehem. Find a man named Jesse who lives there, **for I have selected one of his sons to be my king**." (Emphasis mine.)*

God had already selected one of Jesse's sons to be His king. The choice had already been made. What God had been looking for in His king had already been found in David. Yes, those traits would grow into maturity as the boy would become a man. In David, God had found what Saul was lacking, and He had watched him live it out in the pasturelands and wilderness surrounding Bethlehem.

From reading in 1 Samuel, we find that David spent much of his time tending to His father's flocks. This was his duty assigned by his father, to tend and to protect the family flocks. This could very well have represented a large portion of his family's finances. As the youngest son he would have been watching over the belongings of his father and the inheritance of his other brothers. His own portion would have been small, yet he gave himself to his duty. While he was out in those lonely areas, he would have had ample time to feel sorry for himself or be resentful for how he felt he was treated. He could have slacked off on his duties, doing the minimum required to get by while staying in his father's good graces. Instead he worked at what was asked of him in a diligent way, even in the face of danger. It was on those hillsides where no one was there to see or hear him that God was watching and listening.

As we read the Psalms, we see David with a well-developed relationship with God, as he comes to God often to praise Him, thank Him, and at times bare his soul to Him over the anguish he feels, the justice he seeks, or the forgiveness he needs. I believe that the roots of this relationship were grown on those hillsides, where David learned to play his harp and to sing his praises to God. It was in that wilderness that David's trust in God was forged and strengthened, which is evident from his speech to King Saul in 1 Samuel 17:33-37 as he prepared to face the Philistine giant Goliath:

> *And Saul said to David, "You are not able to go against this Philistine to fight with him; for you are a youth, and he a man of war from his youth."*

But David said to Saul, "Your servant used to keep his father's sheep, and when a lion or a bear came and took a lamb out of the flock,

I went out after it and struck it, and delivered the lamb from its mouth; and when it arose against me, I caught it by its beard, and struck and killed it.

Your servant has killed both lion and bear; and this uncircumcised Philistine will be like one of them, seeing he has defied the armies of the living God."

Moreover David said, "The Lord, who delivered me from the paw of the lion and from the paw of the bear, He will deliver me from the hand of this Philistine."

David could have easily let the lion or bear take the lamb and report to his father that the lamb was lost and there was little he could do about it. Yet David remained faithful in his character and responsible in his actions as he pursued the predators and retrieved what belonged to his father and his family. He also had placed his trust in God to be with him when he acted. David had proven his loyalty to his father in the face of danger. He had proven his faithfulness to his father and family in his care for the flocks. He had proven his love and honor for God in the ways he conducted himself when no one was there to notice. God, however, had been watching attentively. When it had come time for Him to choose the man whom He would entrust to lead His people, He chose David.

In the same way, God had been watching in Roman occupied Israel, and when it came time to choose a man whom He would entrust to be the earthly father of His own precious Son, he chose Joseph.

Chapter 2

෧Ⅲഝ

MY QUESTION AND
THE SURPRISING ANSWER
I RECEIVED

I can remember that night years ago when I was sitting in my bedroom, unsure of what my future held. I was in my early twenties and had recently become a single dad. Asleep in his bedroom down the hall was my three-year-old son. He was my little buddy, my pride and joy. He looked up to me, and in his eyes I could do no wrong. He relied on me for everything he needed in life, and now I was all he had.

We weren't destitute. We had wonderful friends and family who, despite being miles away, were supportive, caring, understanding, and full of hope for us. I hadn't lost hope either. I just honestly didn't know where to start. My dad was a great dad. He was consistent, loving, wise, and forgiving. Most of all he was a man of integrity and a man of substance. While he didn't talk much about his personal relationship with God, I could see it every day in the way he treated us, treated others, and his commitment to study and prayer. His relationship with God was very precious and personal to him and one I can remember admiring from an early age. As I sat there that night, I found myself wondering what I could do to be that caliber of father for my own son.

I knew that even with the example I had been blessed with in my own father, I needed God's help to understand how to be the kind of dad He wanted me to be for my son. It wasn't enough for me to get by doing it on my own. I needed to know what traits I needed to be the dad my son deserved, and the dad my Heavenly Father would approve of. So I did the one thing I knew how to . . .

I asked. There was nothing flowery or philosophical about it. I simply acknowledged where I was at and asked God to show me what was needed of me to be the dad He desired me to be. What God spoke to my heart took me by surprise.

"You want to know the traits I am looking for in a father? Study the man I chose to be the earthly father for My own Son."

I must admit that I was thrown off by the concept. I didn't think it was wrong; I just had never given Joseph much thought. Certainly he had been handy to have around when Jesus was a baby, but the scriptures really didn't say much about him, and he disappeared from the scene fairly quickly from what is mentioned in the four gospels. From my previous understanding of Joseph, he had been the man who had taken care of Mary and baby Jesus until Jesus was old enough to study with the rabbis at the synagogue. He seemed to be the provider and protector until he was no longer needed.

I took the answer I received to heart and studied what I could find out about Joseph. Commentaries differed in their remarks regarding his age, his previous marital status, if he had other children, etc. There were several theories out there, but nothing concrete. A search of the Bible found scriptures mentioned him primarily in select verses in Matthew and Luke. As I meditated on those scriptures, I began to see those characteristics that God had been talking to me about. As I began to look into the culture in his time, I saw the importance of how Joseph's attitude and actions were relevant to my own approach to being a father and how I had much to work toward. Time and experience have shown me that I have by no means arrived in being a perfect dad. I do know that I can attribute the successes I have had in parenting my kids to the lessons the Lord taught me from the life of Joseph and from applying the Word of God to my life as I work toward being more like Jesus.

WHO WAS JOSEPH?

So what about Joseph? I grew up learning that he was from the lineage of King David and that his family was originally from Bethlehem. I had been taught that he was a carpenter by trade, that he was engaged to Mary, and that angels talked to him in his dreams. All in all, it seemed to be a promising life.

Descended from a royal line, a steady vocation, a young wife, and angels came to you in your dreams to help you decipher some of life's larger problems. If only life were so easy! Realistically, he wasn't from a family of great status or wealth. He wasn't a highly educated man by Judean standards; and while his vocation was honorable, it didn't necessarily offer much possibility for upward mobility in society. None of these factors are what caught God's attention when He chose Joseph to be the earthly father for Jesus.

From scripture we can see that in His omnipotence and omniscience God constantly orchestrates things from all angles to accomplish His will. With that in mind, it was apparent to me that Joseph wasn't merely a necessary accessory for Mary in the birth and raising of Jesus. In fact, Joseph wasn't even needed for the conception. Of all the maidens in Israel, God chose Mary. He had examined her heart and measured her commitment and found her worthy to conceive, bear, and raise His Holy Son. I believe that God took that same approach in choosing the man who would have the instrumental role in the Jewish culture of raising and teaching His Holy Son. God chose a *couple* to be the parents of Jesus. He did so knowing their hearts and their attitudes.

In Jewish culture in the time of Jesus, the father was the principal figure in the teaching and discipline of the son. It was the father's responsibility to teach his son of Yahweh, the Torah, the stories from Israel's past, the law and the Talmud. It was the father's responsibility to discipline the son, to enroll him in school, to take him to the synagogue for training, and to teach him a trade. While the mother played a vital role in the upbringing and nurturing of the child, the father was the predominant figure in the preparation of the son for manhood.

Understanding this role, I came to see how vitally important it was that God chose a man whom He had judged to be capable of raising and training His Holy Son from infancy to be the type of man that God had ordained Him to be. This in no way discounts the presence and leading of God in Jesus' life. Jesus was born of a virgin and was sinless. But Jesus was raised by parents who had the fleshly nature still working in their lives, and their ability to live in control of that nature was of paramount importance.

God chose a couple to be
the parents of Jesus. He did so
knowing their hearts and their attitudes.

They made mistakes along the way just as you or I do, but they were diligent to do their best to live their lives dedicated to serving God. God was looking for a mother and father who would teach and model that same diligence to His Son.

Mary and Joseph were not left alone in the raising of this Son, or any of the other children that would follow. God, who gave the child, was there to help them *raise* the child as well. When He placed the child in their care, He did not relinquish all responsibility for the child and walk away. What He did is make them the *caretakers*, the *stewards* of the child—the *PARENTS*.

God does not slink around in the middle of the night, dropping off children on doorsteps and slipping away to never be seen again. Each child has such great value to Him. Each child is His own special creation, a child created with a purpose. His love for each child is so great that He gave a part of Himself in the form of Jesus to be a means of salvation for them. There is no abandonment involved. Rather, there is a delegation of responsibility.

I can remember years ago when my wife told me we were expecting our fourth child. We were excited about the new little one who was on the way. With a son and then two daughters, I was hoping that this baby would be a boy. We could have boys as the bookends. I was really beginning to fantasize about all of the fun things I would do with this little guy. I was in my mid-thirties at the time and was at a different place in life. I had been thinking of the things I could teach this boy and enjoy with him. Just as my oldest son was my little buddy, this new son would be my new little buddy to go with his big buddy of an older brother.

One day my wife went in for a routine checkup and ultrasound and came home with news that I must admit wasn't very welcome in my mind. The pictures were conclusive— that little boy I had been making plans for wasn't in the cards.

The ultrasound had left no doubt that my wife was carrying a little girl.

Now don't get me wrong, I love my daughters, but I was really looking forward to having another boy. Time had proven that I was horrible at doing little girl hair. When your beautiful little six-year-old daughter looks at you with her big brown eyes and says, "It's okay, Daddy. I will do sissy's hair because you do it wrong," you know you have failed remedial hairstyles for preschoolers. My wife would look at them with a frazzled expression on her face as she had to fix my failed attempts at cute little girl hairdos. She was patient with me about it, but it was apparent that of all the things I could do well, this endeavor was a big zero. I was pathetic with pigtails.

I was ready for easy hair combing, wrestling in the floor, playing catch; let's be honest, some testosterone. Having another girl was going to relegate me to living in the estrogen pool for many years to come. This was not the future I had envisioned. In my plan we were supposed to have a little boy and name him Jonathan. He was going to grow to be big and strong. He would love to play baseball and go fishing. He was going to mow my lawn when I got older, climb the ladder to hang the Christmas lights, and move the furniture at Mom's whim. Now all of this had changed. As I was walking through our house one morning bemoaning to myself what I saw as the tragic turn of events, I was addressed by God as sternly as I had ever been in my life. Right in the middle of our living room, I heard these words ringing in my spirit:

"I don't want to hear you whining about this anymore. She is My little girl, My daughter first. I am placing her in your care to love and raise in My ways."

I stopped in my tracks. The tone in which this was spoken to me was stern, disappointed, and not open to questioning. At that moment I understood that my attitude was all wrong. Here my wife and I were in the middle of a beautiful thing, the miracle of life. With so many couples struggling to conceive a child, we were blessed to have this little girl growing in her mother's womb. Here I was selfishly whining about not getting the gender of child I was wanting. I had to be honest with myself and God—I had never once asked Him what His plan was for this child. I had never once asked Him if there were things He wanted to tell me regarding the pregnancy. I had spent all of my time coming up with my own ideas and then telling Him how I would like it.

As I stood there in what was only several seconds, but it seemed like minutes, I realized how far off I had gotten in my priorities. I repented then and there and asked God's forgiveness for whining and being self-centered, and pledged myself to treasure the little girl He had given us. As He had said, she was *His* little girl first.

Every Child Is His First

In reality, every child that is born was and is His first. It's a principle we should be very mindful of. There is an accountability that we as parents have to God. It's not only based on how we conduct ourselves in raising our children, but also in how we look at and treat that child who *still* belongs to Him. He hasn't given up ownership.

The wonderful side to this is that because they still belong to Him, because He still retains ownership of them, because He still wants to be involved in their life, we can call on Him to help us in raising them, caring for them, teaching them, and providing for them. As parents we can become active partners with Him in bringing them up in the love and admonition of God, just as Mary and Joseph did with Jesus.

With that in mind, imagine being given the responsibility of raising God's own Son. We see that from the beginning God was intimately involved with the care for His Son and for providing Mary and Joseph with what they needed to raise Him as God desired. We also see that Mary and Joseph were open to God's guidance. They understood that they weren't left all alone in the journey. Neither are we.

It's in this knowledge that we can take comfort—that God still wants to be intimately involved in the life of the child that we are blessed with. The circumstances under which the child was conceived have not caused God to love that child any less. I think that bears repeating: **The circumstances under which the child was conceived have not caused God to love that child any less.** Somewhere along the line we've gotten the notion that the circumstances a child is conceived in has a direct impact on how much God loves that child. He may disapprove of the circumstances, even detest them—but that innocent child that resulted from those circumstances He still loves deeply—deeply enough to have come in a mortal body and died on a cross for that child.

I bring this up because someone may be reading this book and saying to themselves: "Well, my child wasn't conceived in any manner or situation that could ever be confused with being holy. This all sounds well and good, but it's different in my case."

True, your circumstances may be light years away from the account of Jesus' conception, but your circumstances don't determine God's intent or capacity to love in the midst of them. His desire to come alongside of you to help you care for and raise your child is the same as it is for someone who has gone about things "the right way."

Don't allow yourself to become so hung up on how things *came to be* that you become jaded and give up looking with hope on how things *can be*. If you allow God to have a predominant place in your life and ask Him to help you care for and raise your child, He will meet you where you are and help you get to where He has for you.

That's what He did with Mary and Joseph. They had very few answers on how they were to deal with their own situation. Where they found themselves was in circumstances that had shattered multiple religious and social mores. They were the subject of gossip and ridicule in their own town. In the midst of it all, God was there to help them.

If you've found yourself in need of help in raising your child, God is ready, willing, and able to be that help to you. You are caring for His child, and He will come alongside of you to provide wisdom, strength, and hope. He was there when that child was conceived, formed in the womb, and born into this world—and He has remained even to this very moment.

You are His child as well. He's never stopped loving you or desiring to care for you. You may have a relationship with Him, hopefully a close one, but possibly a casual one. It could be that you may not have a relationship with Him because you don't think He could love or care for you. You may not want a relationship with Him and choose to go in the opposite direction whenever the subject of God or His Son Jesus come up. Here's the thing, He loves you deeply in any of those places. **Your current regard for Him isn't the deciding factor on how He feels about you.**

Romans 5:7-8 says:

> *For scarcely for a righteous man will one die; yet perhaps for a good man someone would even dare to die.*
>
> *But God demonstrates His own love toward us, in that while we were still sinners, Christ died for us.*

It's time for you to reach out and respond to the love and help that God desires to give to you. As you'll find in the following pages, that was the approach Joseph took as he faced a life turned upside down. That love and help that he found in God provided him the strength to face life's challenges head-on, and to come through those challenges not only as a survivor, but as a winner.

Chapter 3

୬ⅢⅢ৩

JOSEPH IN THE
REAL WORLD

The Christmas story is known to many, whether from the simplest of details to a more in-depth verse by verse recounting from the New Testament books of Matthew and Luke. I have to admit that I had read the story many times and heard it many more. I could recite the main events of the story from memory and knew several Christmas hymns and carols to supplement as needed. What I came to understand in studying the story of Joseph is that during my younger years, I had been taught well regarding the details of the Christmas story, but in some respects it was a larger than life story I had never taken the time to consider the real life implications it held for those involved.

The Christmas story is a wonderful recounting of the love of God for you and me, of how He sent His Son to be born into this world in a lowly state. He did this so that He could live as we do, face the same temptations and trials as we do, and ultimately give His life to reconcile us to God. The miraculous events are not window dressing but are essential to the details of God's plan.

In the midst of this plan are a man and woman who accept the assignment of God to become the earthly parents to His Son. They are asked to bring the child into the world, care for Him, and raise Him as their own. But this child wasn't being born into a fairy tale land; He was being born into the real world, a world where the Roman Empire held sway, where society and the local culture had definite expectations. The law of the Jewish religion was well ingrained into the fabric of their culture, and with it were both blessing and consequence. This was the world that Mary and Joseph found themselves bringing God's holy child into, and they were facing the repercussions of the events that would unfold.

When I read through the story again and began to educate myself on the cultural significance of their decisions and actions, it unlocked a new perspective of what they were dealing with and a deeper admiration for them. Looking at Joseph through this new lens, I came to a new level of appreciation of his qualities. He made some very tough choices that didn't put him in the best light in the eyes of others, but his willingness to obey God and handle himself in a godly manner are precisely what brought God's gaze and approval upon him.

In Matthew, chapter 1, we are introduced to Joseph. As the first verses of the passage follow the Jewish system in giving Joseph's genealogy, we find a continuity of lineage from Abraham through David all the way to Joseph. From this line traced from Abraham we see many familiar names— Isaac, Jacob, Ruth, David, Solomon, Hezekiah— illustrating the lineage that Joseph himself could trace his roots. This was not an ordinary lineage, and while there are no passages that denote any significant standing for Joseph, one would venture to believe that this was a lineage that his family looked back on with honor.

To be a Jew who could trace his ancestry back through David and to Abraham was not a light matter. Most of all it speaks of a line of men who had been used of God. Granted, some of those names have much less luster than others, but many are revered for their faith and obedience to God. In his own way, Joseph joined that list of those who were faithful and obedient as well.

In Luke, chapter 1, the angel Gabriel visits Mary and declares to her that she has found favor with God and has been chosen to conceive and bear the Messiah. He then explains to her that this conception will be achieved without the involvement of a man. She would not be conceiving this child by Joseph in marriage, but instead she would be conceiving this child by the miraculous work of the Holy Spirit. Even in the face of what seemed to be impossible and the consequences that would arise from it, Mary yielded herself to the will of Almighty God, responding to the angel, *"Behold the maidservant of the Lord! Let it be to me according to your word"* (Luke 1:38).

Luke 1:26-38 says this:

Now in the sixth month the angel Gabriel was sent by God to a city of Galilee named Nazareth, to a virgin betrothed to a man whose name was Joseph, of the house of David. The virgin's name was Mary.

And having come in, the angel said to her, "Rejoice, highly favored one, the Lord is with you; blessed are you among women!"

But when she saw him, she was troubled at his saying, and considered what manner of greeting this was.

Then the angel said to her, "Do not be afraid, Mary, for you have found favor with God.

And behold, you will conceive in your womb and bring forth a Son, and shall call His name Jesus.

He will be great, and will be called the Son of the Highest; and the Lord God will give Him the throne of His father David.

And He will reign over the house of Jacob forever, and of His kingdom there will be no end."

Then Mary said to the angel, "How can this be, since I do not know a man?"

And the angel answered and said to her, "The Holy Spirit will come upon you, and the power of the Highest will overshadow you; therefore, also, that Holy One who is to be born will be called the Son of God.

Now indeed, Elizabeth your relative has also conceived a son in her old age; and this is now the sixth month for her who was called barren.

For with God nothing will be impossible."

Then Mary said, "Behold the maidservant of the Lord! Let it be to me according to your word." And the angel departed from her.

Shortly after the visit from the angel, Mary traveled to visit her cousin Elizabeth, who although barren for many years, had recently conceived a child under miraculous circumstances—albeit by natural means with her husband. Mary remained with Elizabeth for roughly three months and then returned to her father's house. (See Luke 1:39-56.)

In Matthew, chapter 1, verses 18-25, we read the next piece of the story:

Now the birth of Jesus Christ was as follows: After His mother Mary was betrothed to Joseph, before they came together, she was found with child of the Holy Spirit (v. 18).

Joseph was betrothed to Mary. I can remember hearing about this in the Christmas story and reading it numerous times over the years, and in my Western cultured American mind-set the word "engaged" readily served as the definition for "betrothed" when I read or heard it. I understood it as an old *King James Version* word, and when I substituted "engaged," it made much more sense. Joseph and Mary were engaged, and before they were actually married, she was found to be pregnant with a child that wasn't Joseph's.

That explanation in itself was enough to establish the general sense of the situation. Joseph was about to marry his fiancée only to have her be pregnant with someone else's child. The situation as it appeared outwardly was that Mary had left town for three months to visit her cousin and had now returned pregnant. She was not accusing anyone of assaulting her and causing this condition. There had been no crime committed against Mary. All indications were that this had happened with her knowledge and consent.

Now Joseph is faced with feelings of betrayal, hurt, etc. You've probably heard of a situation like this in your present-day life, whether it's happened to someone close to you or something you've heard of in passing. In most cases, the betrayed party breaks off the engagement and the two go their separate ways. I don't think we could blame Joseph for doing the same. What is interesting in this situation is what comes up in the following verse, verse 19: *"Then Joseph her husband, being a just man, and not wanting to make her a public example, was minded to put her away secretly."*

"Then Joseph her husband." What happened to Joseph being her betrothed, Joseph being her fiancé? When I was "betrothed" to my wife, I was never called her husband. I was her fiancé, who was counting the days until we were married so that I could be her husband. I'd been exposed to this verse many times, but hadn't really caught this dilemma until I began studying Joseph. Here I had found myself two verses into Matthew's account of him, and I was already grappling with a situation that didn't make sense to what I knew from my life today. I began to dig into the culture during Joseph's time and found some interesting information that brought some clarity to the situation.

In the Jewish culture, betrothal, although the marriage had not yet been consummated, was considered as legal and binding on both sides. During the betrothal period, the betrothed woman was set aside for her husband and stayed in her father's house for a period of time until the husband came to take her into his own home. At that time the marriage would be consummated, and the wife would remain with the husband.

This betrothal could not be broken but by a regular divorce. In fact, a breach of this contract was considered as a case of adultery, even though the marriage had not yet been consummated. To add even more gravity to the situation, according to the Mishna, adultery during the betrothal period is a more serious sin than adultery after marriage. We find in Deuteronomy 22:22-24 that this breach was punishable by public exposure of the charges against the person followed by death via stoning.

This newfound knowledge put the events described in the first chapter of Matthew in a whole new light. Joseph and Mary weren't just "engaged," as I understood things to be. They were the same as what I would consider to be married today. With this in mind, let's look back at Matthew 1:19 again:

Then Joseph her husband, being a just man, and not wanting to make her a public example, was minded to put her away secretly.

We now understand how Joseph her betrothed in verse 18 is also able to be considered her husband in verse 19. Notice the next thing said about him, "Being a just man." Even though he was her husband and she apparently had sexual relations with another man and conceived a child before ever consummating her marriage with him, Joseph did not want her to face the public humiliation and death sentence it would bring. Because of that, he "was minded," which could be rendered "had considered things and came to a place of action." After Joseph had considered the situation, along with the possible outcomes and their circumstances, he decided to put Mary away secretly. This would have involved divorcing her privately without assigning any cause, that her life might be saved. As the offense was against him, Joseph had the right to pass on from pursuing the punishment prescribed by the law if he chose to.

He did this because of the first trait that we see of him, that he was a just man.

The term "just" denotes someone who goes about things in a righteous or just manner. It describes someone who not only does things according to the law, but does them with an

JOSEPH IN THE REAL WORLD

approach that is mindful of God's ways. This man not only understood rules and regulations and the judgment associated with them, but he also understood the virtues of mercy and compassion that existed as well. It was this mind and heart that "were minded" to be merciful to Mary in the situation they found themselves in. You must remember, Joseph came to the decision to put Mary away quietly BEFORE the angel appeared to him in a dream to validate Mary's explanation of her pregnancy. Joseph's decision showed a man of prudence, mercy, and compassion.

Joseph was dealing with a perceived betrayal that shattered his dreams of a wife and a family, as well as the stigma of having this happen against him as a betrothed husband. Even facing this, he found a place in himself to put away feelings of the need to get back at Mary for what she had done to him. We see in Joseph's handling of the situation that he was a man who was not easily manipulated by his feelings. His response displays a strong measure of self-control. The man who confronted this situation and came to this conclusion was a man who did not allow his emotions to legislate his actions. The emotional turmoil he must have faced and dealt with did not move him to react with rage, bitterness, a desire for vengeance, or pursuing a means of protecting his reputation at a cost to others. He found a place in himself to look past what this would do to his future and take into consideration the future of Mary and the child she was carrying. He looked beyond himself to come to the conclusion he did when he "was minded."

When God was looking for a man to be the earthly father of His Holy Son, He was looking for a just man, a man who followed not only the law but the heart of the one who gave it. He found this in Joseph.

Matthew 1:20-21 describes to us the following:

But while he thought about these things, behold, an angel of the Lord appeared to him in a dream, saying, "Joseph, son of David, do not be afraid to take to you Mary your wife, for that which is conceived in her is of the Holy Spirit.

And she will bring forth a Son, and you shall call His name Jesus, for He will save His people from their sins."

As Joseph was contemplating the timing and means of putting Mary away secretly, an angel of the Lord appeared to him in a dream, addressed him personally, and validated Mary's story regarding how she had become pregnant. The angel then confirmed to Joseph the identity of this child and charged him with the name that he as the father should give Him.

I can remember hearing and reading this for years and regarding it as some necessary background material that illustrated that an angel appeared to Joseph and told him what to do. Too often Joseph seemed like one of those red uniformed security officers in the old Star Trek series. He was necessary for the plot line so he was shown in a few scenes in which he took orders, and then soon after he was removed from the story

—usually killed by an alien or lost in a cataclysmic galactic mishap. In going back over these passages and breaking them down, I discovered Joseph was much more, and this passage was pivotal to that change in thinking.

We see in verse 20 that an angel of the Lord appeared to Joseph in a dream. That in itself is important, as in it we see that Joseph at some level was sensitive to the things of God. While we do not know if this had ever happened to Joseph before, we can see from the passage that he was open to it and attentive to the details the angel presented. This was not a dream that was discounted as foolish or unrealistic. It was not a dream explained away as the result of eating too much food before bedtime. Joseph regarded the dream and its message as from God, of God, and a divine answer to his unsettling situation.

In the dream the angel addresses Joseph by name and calls him by his lineage,

"Son of David." He wasn't "sinful man," "a chosen man," or merely "son of David." He was "Joseph, son of David." God called him by name. God acknowledged his heritage.

This was personal. God was choosing to engage Joseph in a way that said to him, "I know who you are, where you come from, and what that means." He had paid attention to Joseph and was sending His messenger to address Joseph about God's call and plan for his life.

As we have discussed, Joseph has had to confront the situation where his betrothed Mary has returned from visiting her cousin Elizabeth only to be found with child from someone else.

God was choosing to engage Joseph in a way that said to him, "I know who you are, where you come from, and what that means."

When I look at the situation Joseph was faced with, there are three major options in handling the situation:

- The first would be for him to wash his hands of Mary and allow her to be dealt with as was prescribed by Jewish law.

- The second would be for him to put her away in a discreet manner, absolving himself of the marriage arrangement and allowing them to go their separate ways and move on with their lives. His love for her, in spite of the situation, would be a major factor in choosing this course of action.

- The third would be for Joseph to carry through with the marriage and take Mary and her child into his home. This would have been very difficult for Joseph to do. How he could trust her, even while loving her deeply, would be a major issue in their relationship. Could he allow himself to be put in the same situation again and have his heart broken once more?

After contemplation, he has decided to put her away privately in order to spare her life and the life of her child. He can no longer see himself taking her into his home as his wife, as she has been unfaithful and he has lost his trust in her. Even though he may still love her deeply, he cannot foresee a future between them given the severity of the betrayal and the outlandish story she had told him regarding her pregnancy.

The angel then <u>tells</u> him the following: "*Do not be afraid to take to you Mary your wife, for that which is conceived in her is of the Holy Spirit. And she will bring forth a Son, and you shall call His name Jesus, for He will save His people from their sins*" (Matthew 1:20-21). The angel's words went to the heart of the issue Joseph was struggling with—a fear of what taking Mary in his home and having her as his wife might bring. The angel then validates the seeming outlandish story that Mary had told Joseph regarding her pregnancy.

It was as if the angel were saying, "*Joseph, don't be afraid to take Mary your wife into your life completely. There is no need for you to fear that she has been unfaithful to you with her mind or body or that she has lied to you about how she has come to be with child. She has indeed conceived a child by the mighty work of the Holy Spirit. What could be perceived as betrayal in fact is a blessing to you both, as you have been chosen to be the parents of He who will save His people from their sins. This child is the blessed Messiah that has been foretold by the prophets. When the child is born, you, Joseph, will give him the name 'Jesus.'*"

After the angel had finished delivering the message from the throne room of God, Joseph accepted what he had been told and acted upon it as we see in verses 24 and 25:

Then Joseph, being aroused from sleep, did as the angel of the Lord commanded him and took to him his wife, and did not know her till she had brought forth her firstborn Son. And he called His name Jesus.

Joseph, being roused from sleep, did as the angel had commanded *and took to him his wife.* The angel's message had a profound effect on him. First, it showed him that God was directly involved in the events he was facing. Second, it showed him that God was keenly aware of who he was and what he was being asked to do. God took the time to dispatch an angel to deliver a personal message to Joseph to resolve questions in his heart regarding Mary and her pregnancy. This wasn't a simple visit with a stern command to do what he was told or else. The words the angel delivered did involve a command, but one that was framed in recognition of Joseph's internal struggle and answers to help him overcome it.

What the angel asked of him had consequences. The message the angel delivered also contained peace—a peace that could be held onto in difficult times.

Joseph's response was obedience and trust. The scripture tells us that he returned to Mary and *"took to him his wife,"* which denotes that he took her from her father's home and into his own home to live as his wife. In the eyes of those around them, they were living as a completed husband and wife.

Let's put this in perspective, as it's so easy to gloss over the repercussions this had. To those who had knowledge of Mary's condition, Joseph's taking of her into his home had the possibility of being scandalous. Here's a man who is betrothed. His betrothed leaves town to visit a relative, comes back, and is later noticeably with child. At some point it could no longer be hidden. People would have known that Mary was pregnant as her womb grew in size. Through this, Joseph doesn't accuse her of infidelity.

He doesn't say that she has had a moment of indiscretion, yet he will take her anyway.

There is no attempt to protect his reputation at Mary's expense. Instead he takes the pregnant young woman into his home and treats her as if he was the one involved in the situation.

Joseph's actions would cause him to be presumed guilty by association. The gossip would surely spread throughout Nazareth . . .

"Surely she must be carrying Joseph's child if he has taken her into his home."

"Surely Joseph is a man lacking self-control for Mary to have ended up as she has."

"There go Joseph and Mary. See how large she is getting? Can you believe how depraved they must be to have committed such sin? And coming from a priestly family no less."

"Joseph seemed to be such a fine man, but look at how he's conducted himself. It goes to show you that you can't always trust what you see."

The effect on Mary would have been just as bad. Questions about her virtue or lack of were no doubt brought up. This is the reality of the situation they willingly followed God into. This was a somewhat scandalous beginning to the family reputation that would follow Joseph, Mary, and Jesus in life.

So here Joseph is, the man who seems to lack proper self-control since he got his betrothed pregnant before they had followed proper protocol and law to consummate their marriage. This is the stigma he faces, yet it couldn't be farther from the truth:

Then Joseph . . . took to him his wife, and did not know her till she had brought forth her firstborn Son . . ." (Verses 24-25).

That Joseph *did not know her* means he did not have intercourse with her. Joseph laid next to the woman he loved night after night, surely desiring her, but he controlled those desires because he knew the importance of the child she carried and the responsibility they had both been given. The man who supposedly "couldn't wait," according to gossip, actually waited months to be physically intimate with the woman he loved.

What is so impressive about this is not that Joseph practiced discipline and self-control in how he related to Mary during this time. It's why he did so. We have no indication that the angel threatened his life if he touched Mary. What the angel did tell him was that the child that was conceived and living in Mary was placed there by the Holy Spirit. It was a HOLY CHILD. Joseph understood what "holy" meant. He had a reverence for the things of God, and in his culture the fear of the Lord and the respect for His holiness were strong.

In Joseph's time scribes would wash and purify themselves before even writing the name of God. They understood that the things of God were holy. The Jews of the day understood that those things that were of God were not to be treated lightly and dishonored. Joseph would have been brought up with this understanding, and his reverence for God would have been directly related to his approach to Mary during her pregnancy. Joseph would have been familiar with the words of the prophet Isaiah who had foretold:

> "Behold, the virgin shall conceive and bear a Son, and shall call His name Immanuel" (Isaiah 7:14).

The *virgin* would be with child and give birth. Joseph's care and respect in handling his physical relationship with Mary during her pregnancy and the birth of Jesus were a product of his reverence for the things of God. This would be a key trait that God would want His Son to grow up observing and being taught to follow: Reverence.

The real world isn't always a fun place in which to live. There is sickness, fear, and poverty. There are self-serving people, liars, and gossips. There is famine, war, and death. Mary and Joseph didn't marry and have a family while living in a bubble. There was no sitcom life with warm weekly episodes. They brought a child into the world under scandalous circumstances, later having to flee to a foreign country because the child they had was sought after to be hunted and killed by order of a king driven by paranoia. This series of events had all the makings of a modern thriller. Intrigue, danger, and suspense were at play for this young family.

As I came to understand the setting in which Mary and Joseph found themselves, I found myself actually gaining comfort with the realization that they had it rough just as you and I sometimes do. God's involvement in their lives and situation made the difference in their success in spite of the circumstances. There was hope for me in my situation, and by seeking God to help me, I had come to the right place. Just as Joseph received other worldly solutions to his real world problem, I could, too.

Chapter 4

❦

THE IMPORTANCE
OF GODLY PARENTS

Have you ever wondered if it was important for Jesus' parents to be godly people, or if He was born knowing everything in every situation? In my case, my curious mind wanted to know. In studying about Joseph, I felt the question begged to be asked and hopefully answered . . .

Why Was it Important for Jesus to Have Godly Parents to Raise Him?

As we've already discussed, God was looking for parents who would teach His Son the things most dear to His heart. The man who would serve as Jesus' earthly father would need to possess character and traits that God not only approved of but that were also in line with what He desired Jesus to know and to experience.

This was not an orphanage situation where the child would be looked after by caregivers. God wanted His Son to experience family dynamics, to understand the love of a mother and the love of a father. These experiences would shape His understanding of what each role involved, how they should be carried out, and more than anything else, the different facets of humanity they represented. His time on earth as a man exposed Him to a wide spectrum of emotions, situations, dilemmas, and decisions. This we are given reference to in Hebrews 2:18 NLT:

Since he himself has gone through suffering and testing, he is able to help us when we are being tested.

"Since he himself has gone through. . . ." He was not merely made aware of, or been given examples in great detail of suffering and testing as you and I face. He Himself has gone through suffering and testing. He has experienced them firsthand, just as you and I do. Because He has experienced them firsthand and dealt with them, *"He is able to help us when we are being tested."*

We read further in Hebrews 4:15 NLT:

This High Priest of ours understands our weaknesses, for he faced all of the same testings we do, yet he did not sin.

Jesus faced all of the same testings that we do, yet He did not sin. He faced the situations that we do in our everyday lives in His own life. Jesus lived on this earth for thirty years *before* He began His earthly ministry. Think about that—think of all the things you have experienced in your life. For most people, by the time they have reached the age of thirty that would encompass every emotion and opportunity for a response.

The situations may differ from one person to the next, but mistreatment of different kinds still affects the same basic emotions and decisions on how to respond. Peer pressure can be in different forms, but the pressure to compromise is the same basic root. Jesus was not insulated from these things in some divine cocoon while He lived out His life. He was exposed to them by divine design so that He could not only relate to us and our testings, but that He could also overcome them on our behalf and provide Himself as a perfect example, a sinless man who did not stray from the things of God, but lived them out to the death. By this He could be our Savior.

Jesus would face numerous situations that would test His resolve, His obedience, and His goodness. He would need excellent examples to provide Him the building blocks needed to fulfill His divine call. It was vitally important that Jesus grew up in an atmosphere that taught Him and modeled for Him the correct way to go about life: relationships with others, integrity, character, right thinking as shaped by God's Word, and most importantly, His relationship with God.

Why was Jesus so sensitive to God? There is no question that being God's Son was a major factor. It is also important to note that He had witnessed Joseph and Mary as they lived in reverence of God, and as a result, He grew in His own understanding of His relationship with His Heavenly Father. He then grew into His call, the mission, and His destiny. Jesus' life was lived as a man, and His development would follow the same course of every man or woman—from childhood to adulthood. What He was taught would have an impact on how He saw the world and functioned in it, just as it does with you and me.

When Jesus came into this world, He did so as a child in human flesh. He entered this world with the *ability* to sin, but not with the *predisposition* to sin that you and I have.

How the Sin Nature, or Predisposition to Sin, Entered Mankind

In Genesis, chapter 2, we read where Adam was placed in the Garden of Eden to tend and watch over it. He was told that nothing in the Garden was off limits except for one thing—the tree of the knowledge of good and evil. If he ate of the tree, he was sure to die. Everything else was his to enjoy, just not that particular tree. God even explained why, that if he ate of that fruit, he was sure to die. It was a warning based upon concern for Adam's well-being.

Genesis 2:15-17 NLT says:

> *The Lord God placed the man in the Garden of Eden to tend and watch over it. But the Lord God warned him, "You may freely eat the fruit of every tree in the garden—*

except the tree of the knowledge of good and evil. If you eat its fruit, you are sure to die."

In Genesis, chapter 3, we read where the serpent comes to the Garden and entices Eve to eat of the fruit of the tree of the knowledge of good and evil. As the serpent brings into question God's motives for giving the warning about the tree, Eve gives in and takes a fruit from the tree and eats of it. She then hands the fruit to Adam who eats of it as well.

In 1 Timothy 2:14 we are told that Adam was not deceived. When Adam took and ate of the fruit of the tree of the knowledge of good and evil, his action disregarded God's specific instruction. In eating of the tree, he entered into a "knowledge" of evil. Up to this point Adam had only a knowledge of good—an intimate joining and interaction with what is good—a place where he walked and conversed with God *in His presence.* He had an intimate relationship with the goodness of God. He already knew good.

All the tree had to offer him was the knowledge of evil, not just a wealth of information regarding what was evil, but an intimate joining and interaction with what was evil. When Adam ate of the fruit of the tree, that evil became a part of who Adam was. That evil that became part of Adam brought into his life a predisposition to do what goes against what God had said. It introduced him to a life of sin.

God had instructed Adam and Eve not to eat of the tree because He knew the destruction it would bring to their lives.

Good and evil existed then, they exist today, and they will exist tomorrow. What God did was relegate that knowledge of evil to a singular place in the Garden and warned Adam and Eve to have nothing to do with the fruit of the tree. He didn't forbid them to look at the tree. He made sure they knew it existed in the Garden, but it was to be left alone.

In essence, what God told them was not to take of and ingest what the tree had to offer. What the serpent had persuaded Eve as something God was jealously withholding from her was, in fact, what God wanted to protect her from.

When Adam, as the representative of mankind, ate of the tree, he fell to a place where there now lived inside him a predisposition to things that were contrary to the ways of God. That knowledge—that intimate joining to disobedience and evil that he had acquired—now became a hungry dog inside of him that fought to be fed. This same sad state passed down to all mankind from Adam.

God had instructed Adam and Eve
not to eat of the tree because
He knew the destruction
it would bring to their lives.

Every person after Adam has been predisposed to go against God's ways and words. This was the reason why there was no man who was to be the biological father of Jesus. That sinful nature, that predisposition to go against the things of

THE IMPORTANCE OF GODLY PARENTS

God that would have been passed on from the father, did not exist in Jesus. Mary conceiving by the Holy Spirit circumvented that issue.

While Jesus did not possess this inherent *predisposition* to sin and to go against God's ways, He did possess the *ability* to go against God's ways. While He was sinless, He did face situations on a daily basis that afforded the opportunity to sin. Just as Adam was a sinless man who made a conscious choice to go against the directives and ways of God, Jesus was also a sinless man. In fact, it was that ability to make those choices that Satan attempted to exploit when he came to the wilderness to tempt Jesus. We read of this in Luke, chapter 4:

Luke 4:1-2 NLT states:

> *Then Jesus, full of the Holy Spirit, returned from the Jordan River. He was led by the Spirit in the wilderness,* **where he was tempted by the devil for forty days.** *Jesus ate nothing all that time and became very hungry.* (Emphasis mine.)

Notice that Jesus was in the wilderness and was tempted by the devil for forty days, and during that time He ate nothing. He was on a forty-day fast in an arid place where wild animals roamed. This wasn't the classic tree-filled wilderness like the Yukon. This was the Judean desert. Day after day you grow hungrier, thirstier, and more weather-worn from the elements. It is hot in the daytime and cold at night. In the night air, you hear sounds of dangerous animals prowling in the darkness outside of your field of vision. There would have been the temptation to find something to eat, or to return to civilization before you became a lion's meal. Through this time, Jesus remained disciplined and maintained His fast.

Then after forty days a being appears to Him and says the following:

> *Then the devil said to him, "If you are the Son of God, tell this stone to become a loaf of bread."*
>
> *But Jesus told him, "No! The Scriptures say, 'People do not live by bread alone'"* (Luke 4:3-4 NLT).

In that time of weakness Satan sought to get Jesus to depart from what God would have Him do. Was this attempt and the tempting of the last forty days Satan merely going through the motions, or did he have an expectation that this could work?

He had tempted sinless Adam and watched him give in and fall into sin. He had enticed sinless angels into a rebellion in heaven, and a third of the angels followed him in his rebellion against God. He was pulling out all the stops to entice Jesus to do the same. He had no guarantee that it would work, but he knew the ability to sin was there.

Thankfully Jesus resisted Satan's questioning of God's Word by answering from that same Word to refute him, turning back Satan and his temptations. He continued that path all the way to His death on the cross. There were many opportunities to take the easy way out and to deviate from

God's instructions and plan. Yet He did not depart from what He knew was right in God's eyes.

In Proverbs 22:6 KJV we read the following:

Train up a child in the way he should go: and when he is old, he will not depart from it.

Train up a child in the way he should go, with the end result to be that when that child becomes a man and lives his life, he will remember those things that he was taught and will keep them. They will be a guiding force in his life. The book of Proverbs has several passages that address what benefits a life of following and obeying God would bring. As devout Jews, Mary and Joseph would have been well versed in these scriptures and the promises they contain. They would have been diligent to impart them to their children.

Why was it so important that Mary and Joseph were godly parents who taught a reverence of God and the things of God? It was because they would be the primary instructors of young Jesus in the ways of God—the way He should go. They would be living these things out in front of Him on a daily basis, providing a solid foundation for Him to build upon and develop in as He grew into manhood. The days would come when He would be under intense pressure, and the temptations would come to try to sway Him into disobedience to God.

As Jesus faced the temptations from Satan in the wilderness, Jesus did not depart from the way He was to go but instead answered each of Satan's attempts to try to sway Him by responding with scripture—scriptures and their related stories that He would have learned as a boy, those scriptures and stories that He would have learned from His parents.

Chapter 5

☙

GOD'S CHARACTER TRAITS IN JOSEPH

As you narrow the list of candidates to be a parent to your children in your place, there is one particular factor that is dominant. This person whom you will be choosing to act in your place has many things to measure up to, but along with those traits, you need that person to respect who you are and what you stand for. You want that person to love your children as you would love them. You want that person to respect the love you have for them and remember how much you treasure them. This person is not to be your replacement, but he is to be your representative. He is to portray your greatest desires for your children to them, be their shoulder to cry on, their stable, solid person in life who gives of himself to them as you would.

The reality is that if the person you or I considered didn't respect who we are and what our desires were for our children, then they would be a poor choice to carry on what we desired to see instilled into our children's lives. Even if "Bob" and I agreed on 99 percent of the same morals, principles, and parenting techniques, yet he didn't respect my place as their father and all the ways I desired to be that to them, he would go about them in his own manner with little regard to what I would approve of. How he conveyed those things and how he thought and acted on a daily basis would be done without respect to my wishes or ways.

A good example of this would be in how a child is taught the importance of telling the truth. One parent can approach the subject by confronting the child caught lying and explaining to him how it is wrong—followed by making them wash his mouth out with soap. While that may not be politically correct today, it was a regular punishment in times past. Another parent might set the child down and have them write "I will not lie" one thousand times on sheets of paper. Another parent might explain to them that lying is wrong, and then attempt to reason with the child to help them understand the concept.

All three of these approaches have been used in dealing with the situation. Now be honest with yourself—as you read them, which one sounded most like how you would handle the situation and which one was furtherest from what you would approve of? As you do so, you can see the importance of choosing the person who would best represent who you are and how you would do things. You've already found that the person agrees that lying is wrong and that the children should be taught not to lie, but how they accomplish it in your place is just as important to you as that they teach it.

It was the same with God as He searched for the man whom He would choose to raise His Son. This man not only had to be in agreement with what God had to say, but he also had to respect God in such a deep way that he would act in ways that were of God's own character. He had to revere God beyond just his thoughts; this reverence had to be something that was at the core of who he was. This man's principles and his motivation would have to be based on who God was to him. From that place, all of his thoughts and actions would be governed.

This man wouldn't be perfect, but it would already be working in him to strive to walk as righteously as he could before God. Proverbs 7:9 NLT says, *"For you look deep within the mind and heart, O righteous God."*

When God looked deep within the heart and mind of Joseph, he saw His own character traits in development. His examination showed that this man was living his life with a conscious effort to do things in a way that would be pleasing to God. His thoughts and actions were being governed by the principles of God, and he had proven this in his dealings with situations and people. This wasn't a man who was merely well learned in the things of God. This was a man who was actively pursuing them in his approach to life. He wouldn't be a mere teacher to God's Son; he would be an acceptable model to Him.

In the latter portion of the Apostle Paul's letter to the church in Galatia, he addressed improper and proper behavior for those who love and follow after Jesus. Those who walk after the flesh, or their sinful nature, approach their everyday life in a self-serving manner that is devoid of regard for God and His law. These behaviors go against the nature of God.

On the other side of the equation, Paul discusses what he terms the "fruit of the Spirit." These are traits that are exhibited by a person who follows after God and approaches everyday life by living in a manner not only pleasing to God but motivated and governed by God's ways—His thoughts and motivations. While they are commonly known as the "fruit of the Spirit," I like to refer to them also as the "character traits of God." As they are traits that the Holy Spirit personifies, they are of God Himself. These character traits of God, identified in Galatians 5:22-23 KJV, are as follows:

> *But the fruit of the Spirit is love, joy, peace, long-suffering, gentleness, goodness, faith, Meekness, temperance: against such there is no law.*

When God looked for a man to be a father to His Son, He most assuredly looked for a man who lived a life that was governed and motivated by the things that were most dear to Him. As discussed earlier, this man would see things as God saw them and go about things as God would have them done. This man would have a deep reverence for

God's ways—ones that were played out in his daily life. When God's eyes rested upon Joseph, those traits were scrutinized and found to be acceptable. Joseph was an imperfect man, but among the imperfection God found a man who in thought, word, and deed exhibited those godly character traits that were so precious in His sight.

It was vitally important that Joseph already was operating in this godly approach to life, as the events of his betrothal, marriage, and future life would place a great demand on him. He would need to be stable and solid in them before those events began to unfold, as there would be no time to begin development after the fact. These godly character traits are not instant, and there is no "easy bake" version. They are grown in a person through the passage of time and through trial, cultivated by the Spirit of God in yielded minds and hearts. That God recognized them in Joseph showed that they were not just potential but were already in use with the capacity to grow greater.

With this in mind, let's look back again at Joseph and Mary's story with an emphasis on defining in detail each of the godly character traits listed in Galatians, chapter 5, and then also identifying them as they relate to ways Joseph approached and handled the situations he faced. As we do this, it will give us an even better insight into what God saw in this man who caught His eye and caused Him to choose Joseph to be the earthly father of His Son.

> *Joseph was an imperfect man,*
> *but among the imperfection God found a man*
> *who in thought, word, and deed exhibited*
> *those godly character traits that were*
> *so precious in His sight.*

Note: As different Bible translations can give varying English words for the traits we are discussing, I've chosen to present the *King James Translation* of the verse. When you read words like "meekness" or "temperance" that aren't commonly used in our everyday conversation, it can be difficult to grasp a solid understanding of what these words actually mean. I have accompanied the English word with the Greek word used in the original text that the English word was translated to. My hope is that by doing so, readers will have information to better assist in any study on these words they may choose to pursue. I am not a Greek scholar, yet having these words to study for meaning and usage helped me gain a greater understanding of the traits that come from the Spirit of God and that we are encouraged to develop and walk in.

Let's look again at Galatians 5:22-23 from the *King James Version:*

> *But the fruit of the Spirit is love, joy, peace, long-suffering, gentleness, goodness, faith, Meekness, temperance: against such there is no law.*

LOVE – *AGAPE*

This type of love is the highest form of love, the type of love personified by how God looks at and relates to us. This type of love is not based on what the other party can do in return. It is a love that exists because of the value one assigns to the person on whom the love is placed. This is the love that God has for you and me—for God so loved that He gave—for God valued us so highly that He gave of Himself. He gave knowing there was nothing that you or I could reciprocate that carried any value commensurate with what He was giving. With *agape* love, the giver has no strings attached. This form of love gives in spite of the hurt that may exist, the lack of return that may be present, and the uncertainty of any response. When someone loves in this way, it is a love that is not based on him, but on the treasure he sees the other to be.

Agape love—loving the way God does. It's not something that you can find wherever you look. In today's world so many people are geared toward looking out for themselves, often at the expense of others. We find this in the workplace, in our neighborhoods, and sadly, even in the church.

While *phileo* love, what we more commonly know as brotherly love, does look to the best interests of someone else above our own interests, it does so because of a common bond or care for others. *Phileo* love is a wonderful emotion. It's that love that causes a soldier to take a bullet for his squad mate. It's that love that motivates a person to give an organ to a person in need. It is a precious bond between people, some known, some strangers, that causes us to do things for others in a selfless manner.

Agape, however, goes further in that it seeks to do right regardless of the cost.

Agape is truly selfless because it requires the person to remove self from the equation. Even if there has been harm done by the other party, it causes the person still to act on the offender's behalf. Let's observe that in Joseph's life . . .

Joseph is betrothed to Mary, a status that in our time would be the same as legally married. He has been preparing the home in which they will live, making additions to suit the needs of his new wife while she has been away visiting her cousin Elizabeth. He has been anxiously anticipating her return to Nazareth so that he can see her again and hear her voice.

The day comes when she returns to Nazareth and something seems out of place. He senses that things aren't the same as when she had departed weeks earlier. After meeting with her, he hears the shocking news that she is pregnant, and then hears a crazy story about how there wasn't another man involved. She swears that she was visited by an angel and conceived the child she is carrying by the Holy Spirit. Would you believe this wild tale? How would you react?

There is no doubt that he was hurt and probably bewildered by the turn of events. He may have gone back to that home he was preparing and kicked the chair he had just built for her.

"Why? Why?"

"Why did she have to do this and then tell me this wild story? Does she think me such a fool to believe it?"

In spite of his pain and sense of betrayal, he still withheld himself from taking actions that would have caused her harm or death. Where *phileo* would have surely stepped in to protect an innocent woman, *agape* was at work to hold Joseph back and protect Mary in spite of the harm she had done him. While his heart ached from the betrayal he perceived, she still meant so much to him that he couldn't bear the thought of harm coming to her. While it would cost him in the eyes of others by not making a public show of her actions to vindicate himself, he had come to a place of decision that he would put her away or divorce her as privately as possible so that she would be spared.

We see this godly trait in action in Joseph as he came to his decision with no knowledge of the truth of the events that had taken place with Mary. It was in him to love and to care even if he had the right to be angry, even if he had the right to demand justice for himself. He also had the capacity to love someone in this manner to the point of acting on it. Many people will say they would do these things, but until they are faced with the situation and the heartbreak that comes with it, they don't really know. Joseph came to his decision under extremely difficult circumstances.

God saw this in Joseph and watched it play out in how he cared for Mary from the time they first met until the night that Joseph had to face the news of her pregnancy. As Joseph "did not want to disgrace her publically," he was looking toward her future as well as his. He moved past his own pain to spare Mary the pain that the law prescribed.

By handling the situation in this manner, Joseph also displayed other godly character traits. The gravity of the situation didn't afford him the luxury of only having to act in a godly manner in one area, but like so many of life's surprises, it demanded that he face the situation on several different fronts at once—each personal and difficult. Deep relationships are intricate by nature, and in those intricacies lie multiple layers of thought and response with which we are confronted.

Here is Joseph, in love and preparing to be married. He's just learned from his betrothed who has been away for the past weeks that although she left their village without child, she has now returned pregnant. Then she has told him a very outlandish story about angels and virgin conception. His heart is broken; his mind conflicted. Does he lash out in violence, responding back in retribution? Does he think of himself and the best way to keep his reputation as untarnished as possible? Does he take hold of his right for exposure of her infidelity and public vengeance?

No.

Did these responses cross his mind? Possibly. Did he entertain any of them to the point of acting on them?

No.

Somewhere within himself he made the decision to let the ways and the character of God shape his thoughts and decisions. I've heard it said that you can't stop a bird from flying over your head, but you can stop it from landing on your head and building a nest. Those thoughts may have "flown over" Joseph's head, but by his attitude and actions we can see that he did not allow them to land or roost. You or I can operate in the same way.

So we have Joseph, greatly troubled but motivated by his love for Mary, allowing that love to soften him towards her. Yes, he loved her as a man loves a woman, but he also cared for her with a love that was based upon how much he valued her, beyond the circumstance, knowing that although this love appeared to have been rebuffed in action, he, nonetheless, still maintained it. Past the perceived betrayal and crazy story, he still loved her and cared for her well-being.

As this love moved in him, he contemplated how best to deal with the situation.

Matthew 1:19 states:

"Then Joseph her husband, being a just man, and not wanting to make her a public example, was minded to put her away secretly."

Notice, he was a good (just) man who did not want to disgrace her publicly. We have seen that Joseph was motivated by love for Mary and the God-kind of love (*agape*) at this point. That love served as the basis for how he would then approach the situation as he considered how to handle it. What rose up in him during this time shaped his thoughts and actions, beginning with longsuffering.

Longsuffering – *Makrothumia*

This word can also be translated as forbearance or patience. It carries the meaning of enduring of wrong without becoming quick to anger or thinking of revenge. A person who exhibits longsuffering would be someone who is not easily provoked, a person who has the ability to rein in his emotions and not to act rashly. This is a person we would refer to as having a long fuse.

Joseph, motivated by his love for Mary, moved into a place in his mind where he decided that he would not act in anger or seek revenge. He kept control of himself and held his emotions in check as he tried to understand his situation and the options he had in responding to it. It would have been easy for him to lash out to release his anger or to allow feelings of self-pity to move him to take actions that would have unconsidered consequences. In this situation he had to consider seriously what would be the fate of Mary and her unborn child. He recognized the gravity of the situation and set himself to be mindful of this. As he did so, he operated in meekness.

Meekness – *Prautes*

Prautes is a word that was often used by Greek writers to describe a person's attitude and response in dealing with others. A person who operates in meekness is not a weak person who simply wilts or knuckles under when faced with pressure. A meek person is one who operates from a place of strength, but does not allow that strength to be the overriding factor in how they treat others, even when treated wrongly. Although the meek person has the ability to defend himself strongly and forcefully, he allows gentleness, humility, and longsuffering to have their way in his attitude and use of power. He does not throw his weight around or flex his muscles to assert himself. The meek person is confident in his strength and authority without needing to show it. He understands that "with great power comes great responsibility."

Joseph knew it was in his power to have Mary exposed as being unwed and pregnant. By doing so he could save his reputation and move past the unbelievable turn of events that faced him. Faced with stigma and ridicule, he chose to let his love for Mary guide his use of the power he found himself holding over her welfare and future.

He didn't see this an opportunity to display his righteousness in contrast to hers. Instead he knew that there was a way that the situation needed to be handled that would take more from him than just the love he had for Mary. It would take his moving in that love and making the right decision. As he searched his heart and mind for an answer to the situation, he considered what would be right and just in not only God's law, but also in God's way of doing things. How would God want him to feel and respond in the situation? He would want him to be good and kind.

GOODNESS – *AGATHOSUNE*

The person who exhibits this trait is one who not only tries to do the right thing, but one whose regular disposition is to think right and act right. Goodness in the context of the character traits of God is a deeply held desire to do things that will be pleasing in God's eyes. This goodness is shown in the ways a person goes about his life, and specifically in the treatment of others—giving to meet their needs, lending a helping hand, and going out of his way to make a difference.

The goodness that was in Joseph moved him to seek a way to deal with Mary that would follow not only the provisions of God's law, but also a manner that would be in line with the love that he had for her. It was his desire for her to not come to harm or be placed in great peril.

GENTLENESS/KINDNESS – *CHRESTOTES*

This character trait refers to how a person interacts and handles contact with others. Gentleness or kindness describes a person who refrains from harshness towards others. This person is not prone to being judgmental, instead valuing the other person and attempting to treat others as they would want to be treated.

As Joseph acted in love toward Mary, practicing an attitude of longsuffering and patience toward her, he approached the situation in meekness—knowing that although he was in a position of power in how to deal with her, he did not feel the need to use that power for his own vindication.

The goodness in his heart drew him to a frame of mind that looked to find a solution that would not only honor God's law but also preserve Mary's life. He began to go through the different options in his mind, and the gentleness and kindness that were part of him chose a solution that was permitted by law but also was the least harmful to the woman he loved. Betrayed or not, his love for her was not so shallow that it was easily tossed aside. He saw no relief to him in her harm—only additional sorrow. He came to the conclusion that he would put her away privately, preserving what dignity he could for both Mary in her situation and he in his own. It wasn't an easy decision to come to, but he believed it was the right one.

We don't know if this thought process occurred in just a few hours or possibly several days. In any case, Joseph worked his way through the shock, anger, disbelief, and heartache to come to his decision—a decision filtered through and tempered by the character of God that was operating in his life.

As we read on in the account in Matthew, chapter 1, we read the following in verses 20-22, 24-25 NLT:

> *As he considered this, an angel of the Lord appeared to him in a dream. "Joseph, son of David," the angel said,*

"do not be afraid to take Mary as your wife. For the child within her was conceived by the Holy Spirit.

And she will have a son, and you are to name him Jesus, for he will save his people from their sins."

All of this occurred to fulfill the Lord's message through his prophet . . .

When Joseph woke up, he did as the angel of the Lord commanded and took Mary as his wife.

But he did not have sexual relations with her until her son was born. And Joseph named him Jesus.

While we've previously discussed this passage, let's look at it again in light of identifying the godly character traits at work in Joseph during this time. After careful deliberation, Joseph has settled upon a very discreet approach to handling the situation that will protect Mary and her unborn child while releasing him from a relationship that, although he is shattered to lose, he has no trust in any longer. His future with Mary, whom he loves, is gone, but at least in this way the woman he loves will still live. It is painful to him to see her go, but not as painful as seeing her gone from this world.

As Joseph considers his plan and lies down to sleep on it, he is visited in a dream by an angel where his fears are addressed and he is given specific instruction. He awakes and does as the angel commanded, taking Mary as his wife. That's quite a turn of events in a short amount of time. It's in this quick turn of events that we see more of God's character at work in Joseph.

Put yourself in Joseph's shoes. Your fiancée returns from visiting family out of town to tell you she is pregnant by none other than the Holy Spirit. You are practicing good in thought and feeling as you try to process this all, and then as you think you may have a plan to handle it in a way that preserves the woman you love, you decide to sleep on it. BOOM! In a dream an angel appears and talks to you in great detail about your situation and confirms the seemingly crazy story your fiancée had told you about how she got pregnant. Not only that—he instructs you to go ahead and marry her and to name the child a specific name. By naming this child, you are claiming it as your own. Then you wake up.

Okay, truthfully, are you going to hop up, believe the story, go to her father's house and say "Baby, it's all okay. Let's get married today!" Probably not. At least she might believe you when you tell her about the dream and the angel, but you probably aren't sure yourself. This is what Joseph faced. He's had the dream, and now it is decision time. He went to bed with what he thought was a good, just plan that would be pleasing to God. He wakes up with a totally different plan delivered from the throne of God to him in a spectacular manner. What does he do? He accepts the plan and acts on it. For him to do this, he needed his questions answered and his fears relieved. The angel did this for him in the dream, and in doing so, Joseph was able to move forward in peace.

Peace – *Eirene*

This peace is not a mere feeling of tranquility when all is well but describes a tranquility in spite of the circumstances. This is a peace that allows a person to maintain composure and stability even if the world around him is swirling out of control. This is the peace that Paul understood so well when he wrote his letter to the church in Galatia based in a confidence in God in the midst of adversity—based upon His character and His Word.

This is the peace that Paul spoke of in Philippians 4:7 KJV when he stated that this *"peace of God, which passeth all understanding, shall keep your hearts and minds through Jesus Christ."* This peace that passes understanding is a peace that doesn't make sense to the person who does not have confidence in someone to look after them, a trust in someone able to preserve and deliver them from a situation they are unable to handle on their own. This peace goes beyond the understanding of the natural circumstances and logical outcome. This peace keeps moving forward and passes by natural understanding which has given up and waits for an end it sees as inevitable. This peace is not a place of obliviousness or denial. It is based on a confidence and trust in spite of what the normal outcome would be.

This is the peace that took Jesus to the cross to endure suffering and death on our behalf. Through the pain and anguish of that event, He held onto His trust in His Heavenly Father, and as He breathed His last breaths, He committed

His Spirit into His Heavenly Father's arms. He endured this death because He had a peace that passed any understanding. He believed what God had said about Him, that He would rise again to life. He trusted that His death would bring salvation to millions. He counted Him faithful who had promised.

When we look at the life of Joseph, we see a man who faced events in his life that could shake a person to their core: the perceived betrayal of one you love, the stigma that comes to a man whose betrothed becomes pregnant before their marriage ceremony, the spur of the moment flight to another country to flee death. As Joseph was confronted with these challenges, he ultimately responded to them with a level of composure that so many people wouldn't. In actuality they couldn't. Joseph was surely alarmed and shaken at times, but he was able to arrive at a place of peace in each situation, grounded in what God had said to him and his trust in God to be faithful to those words.

Marrying a pregnant girl who said she had conceived without being with a man didn't make sense. Trusting that she had been faithful when the mental image of her pregnant belly bulging beneath her dress was stuck in your mind—that was a very major stretch of the imagination that didn't seem to have any basis in reality.

This brought Joseph an answer to the questions swirling around his head. It wasn't exactly a realistic answer, as it passed all understanding, but he took it as truth and came to a place of peace that allowed him to do the improbable and take

Mary as his wife, accept the child as his own, and begin a life sure to be full of surprises. He was able to face it all because he learned to find that place of peace in himself where God's presence and His Word held the prominent spot and provided the anchor for his soul.

Having done as the angel instructed, Joseph took Mary as his wife, completing the marriage ceremony and moving her into the home that they would share. With this there is a key item that we need to consider. Notice what we are told in verse 25:

> *"But he did not have sexual relations with her until her son was born . . ."* (NLT).

Joseph did not consummate his marriage with Mary until after her son was born.

In doing so, Joseph practiced temperance.

Temperance – *Enkrateia*

While meekness describes the control a person exhibits in dealing with others, temperance involves the self-control a person maintains in regard to his desires. In 1 Corinthians 7:9 this word is used to describe control over one's sexual desires, while in 1 Corinthians 9:25 it is used to describe an athlete's focus, dedication, and self-control in training for an event. Temperance is not merely turning down that extra slice of pie to watch your weight; it is foregoing the pie to maintain the goal of your eating plan.

A person with the self-control listed in Galatians 5:23 is a person who has worked to attain a level of balance and moderation in his life where his decisions are not based on what feels good, but on what is right. In this context, what is right is defined by what is right in God's eyes. The man of temperance or self-control is not perfect, but he habitually tries to live his life to meet that goal.

As we discussed in chapter 3, Joseph practiced a great deal of self-control in the ways he related to Mary while she was pregnant. Although married, they did not have sexual relations until after the child had been born. This man who had married a pregnant girl, probably thought by many to be a man lacking self-control, had practiced a great amount of self-control over the months following his marriage to Mary. He kept his desire in check because he understood what was right in God's eyes in regard to his situation.

With all of the events leading up to Jesus' birth and then beyond, God was looking for a man who would follow His instructions and hold fast to what had been asked of him. This man would have to be trustworthy on a scale that only God could accurately judge. Not only had this man been trustworthy, but could he be counted on in the future regardless of the circumstances? Was he a man of faith—a faithful man?

Faith – *Pistis*

In the context of this verse in Galatians, it refers to the faithfulness of a person. This person is loyal, dependable, not easily swayed or moved. The faithful person is trustworthy, can be counted on to hold a confidence to keep their word. This person is solid and can be counted on in good times and in bad times. In 1 Corinthians 4:1-2 Paul made it very clear that faithfulness is the chief requirement to be a steward or caretaker, especially of the things of God. We can also see this in God's choice of David as the King of Israel, as in Act 13:22 it is said of David:

> *He raised up for them David as king, to whom also He gave testimony and said, "I have found David the son of Jesse, a man after My own heart, who will do all My will."*

We see this also in Noah, who had found favor in God's sight in the midst of wickedness throughout the earth. After receiving detailed instructions to build a boat to prepare for a flood that was unheard of, we are told in Genesis 6:22, *"Thus Noah did; according to all that God commanded him, so he did."*

Faithfulness is what sets a man apart in God's eyes.

When Joseph was instructed by the angel to take Mary as his wife, he obeyed, knowing well the stigma that would come with it. When the child was born, he named the child Jesus, just as he was instructed, and took the child as his own son in everyone's eyes. Later, Joseph was once again visited by an angel in a dream and instructed to flee Israel and move to Egypt that very night. Once again, Joseph was quick to obey. Obedience to what God asked of him was a characteristic that was strong in Joseph, and it was a precious trait in the eyes of God.

Finally, we come to the godly character trait of joy. I purposefully left it until last because I see it as the trait that had to serve as a constant buoy to Joseph in his life. The details we are given of his life are few but rich, with the trials and probable roller coaster of emotions involved numerous times. What we see in him is an attitude of optimism, of hope in the midst of adversity, and of a desire to see things in the light of God's Word and His character. To function this way in life, one must have joy—God's joy.

Joy – Chara

The Greek word "*chara*" is a derivative of the Greek word "*charis,*" which means "grace," used in scripture to denote the grace of God. More than mere happiness, which comes and goes due to circumstances, feelings, or even hormonal balances, joy is more than a feeling; it is a state of being that one is able to function in due to its nature being based in God's grace. While happiness can be fleeting in hard times, joy can be present in the midst of adversity, as it has its root in God's presence and power to affect one's situation. Happiness is a reaction to the situation at hand. Joy is a buoy of the spirit and soul while one waits expectantly for the answer he is trusting for, for the resolution of a situation in his favor.

As I read the account of Joseph and all he faced, I'm reminded of Nehemiah 8:10,

"The joy of the Lord is your strength" (KJV).

To face all he did and keep moving forward in the plan of God, Joseph had to draw upon a strength beyond his own. I believe that he had learned to draw upon the joy of the Lord during his life, and as he undertook this great calling on his life, he drew from that joy to help him fulfill what had been asked of him. It is no different for you or me today.

Psalm 37:23 KJV says,

"The steps of a good man are ordered by the Lord: and he delighteth in his way."

When I read this story, the providence of God amazes me. Of all the men on the face of the earth, He had located and chose a man for Mary who had these traits working in him at the time she conceived this child out of wedlock. This wasn't just an extremely fortunate turn of events; it was a carefully orchestrated plan set in motion by the hand of God. He chose HIS MAN and HIS WOMAN to bring together, knowing that they had in them the ability to trust Him and walk out this crucial piece of His plan of redemption.

What an awesome thought!

These weren't two star-crossed lovers or a frail young maiden and an old curmudgeon who happened to find themselves caught in the middle of a series of events. They were God's handpicked people! He looked at them both and decided not only that they as individuals had what He desired as parents for His Son, but also that they as a COUPLE had what He desired for His Son. What they would build as a life together was important to God. It ran deeply from the beginning.

Chapter 6

⟨∞⟩

FEELING YOUR WAY
THROUGH THE
MAZE CALLED LIFE

Have you ever been in a funhouse where there was a dimly lit maze? You have a general sense of which way to go, but there are many twists and turns along the way, and the dim light doesn't allow you to see much around you. You often make your way by feeling the walls around you and slowly moving as you follow the contour of the wall. In many ways that's similar to raising children. On our own we are often feeling our way through the maze of life, reacting to our surroundings as we inch along. We know the destination we are heading for will bring us to an end of the maze, but our path is dimly lit, uncertain, and full of surprises.

I can attest that raising my kids has been full of twists and turns. Life itself throws us different situations and circumstances that affect our life and our family. Each child is unique, with his or her own personality. There are so many variables that can enter into parenting each individual child that we are hard pressed to be able to handle them all effectively. That isn't to say we can't, but rather that it isn't an easy task. You can easily validate that by finding a group of parents, and after listening to their description of their family life, give them your explanation of how they should have handled things. You will quickly learn from them that there is much more involved in each situation than a few brief sentences can convey.

Of the many families I've had the pleasure to get to know, I learned that no one had the market cornered on the tranquil, smooth running, uneventful life. As strong as their family was, full of love and commitment, they had struggles they faced.

Being a young father, I was blessed to be involved with men who were older, wiser, and humble enough to share what they had learned in raising their families. The illusion I had of a perfect family was gently brought into perspective by these men who cared enough to share some of the trials they had gone through personally and as a family. These were good men, godly men who lived what they believed. They had great families. They had also gone through tough times in their lives. It all hadn't been smooth sailing, but they had stood together and made it to the other side intact and stronger.

I remember an older man that I grew to know and look up to. Jim was a member of the men's Bible study that I was a part of, and he and his wife Diane had taken my wife and me under their wings. They were a great couple who had raised their family and were moving toward retirement age when Jim had been laid off from his company. My wife and I watched as they took their situation in stride, and instead of complaining Jim dutifully searched for employment and gave the rest of his days to helping with our church building project.

I always appreciated Jim's sense of humor and his smile. Most of all I appreciated his candor with me. As my wife and I would visit Jim and Diane at their beautiful home, we would talk on our way home about how someday we would like to have a great place like they had. We would like to have successful kids like they had. We would like to have cute grandkids like they had. We wanted to be still as loving and playful in our older years as they were with each other. They seemed to be where we wanted to be at their stage in life.

As we would share with them how much we valued their friendship and how we looked to their example, their honesty and humility were such a precious gift to us. They would share with us about the trials they had been through over the years and how things hadn't always gone as smoothly as they appeared. Life had shown them many twists and turns along the way, but their love for each other and their faith in God had seen them through.

It had a great impact on my wife and me as newlyweds. Their kindness and openness helped to ground us for times to come ahead. We learned from them that life itself would be full of changes, but they could be navigated and handled. We also learned from them that parenting wasn't an exact science, and that it was okay not to have all the answers. It was so very reassuring to us to have people who had things together let us know that raising children wasn't something that you could have mapped out with no need to change course or approach. It was something that you had basic standards that you follow, but also learn to be adaptive to each child's personality and needs.

Our son was six when our next child, a little girl, was born. Big changes had come to the Clark household. We had recently moved from Illinois to Oklahoma, and now we had added to our little family. The coming months were full of surprises for us, as we adjusted to a new baby, new family dynamics, and the pressures that come with it all. I'd like to say we handled it all with no problem, but even though we were experienced in caring for a child, we were not experienced with all the new variables we found ourselves dealing with. We were quite literally feeling our way through the maze of parenthood. We weren't clueless, inept parents. We were inexperienced with the new dynamics and the life circumstances we were facing. This was a different version of the balancing act we had grown accustomed to.

We went through a similar experience when child number 3 arrived less than two years later. We hadn't suddenly become idiots at the parenting thing, but we were facing new dynamics. It was as if I had to pause and say, "Hello, baby girl number 2. Pardon me while I reach out to feel the wall to this maze I'm traveling through."

Maybe you can relate to what I'm talking about. You may feel totally inept at this whole parenting thing, or you may feel secure in parenting but are honest enough to admit that you face situations from time to time to which you don't have all the answers. Either is okay to admit to. None of us have all the answers to the various situations we face as we raise children. Many times we react or respond quickly when we have to parent our kids. Sometimes it's warranted. Other times maybe we should have taken a bit of time before we reacted.

I had a wise man tell me years ago, "Raise them the best you know how and trust God to fill in the holes you have." A pretty simplistic approach, but one that honestly is the best I have ever come across.

The first part requires that we actually take the time to be a parent. Not every parent has the ability to be with their children on a daily basis, but here's a key—when you are with them, *be with them!* Not just *physically*, but *emotionally* as well. Think of it this way: to raise something, you are required to have your hands on it and exert energy toward it. If you are truly *raising* your child to a place you desire them to be, your hands and energy will be involved.

For the second part, do it the best you know how. The *best* you know how. It's not enough to give what you have left over after your work and your friends take what they need. Your children deserve *your best*. Now you may look at this and think you don't know much about being a parent and that this child was a surprise you hadn't planned on. Congratulations!

You are part of an expansive group of people who have faced the same situation! Now that we've established that fact, move to finding out what you need to know about being a good parent. If you don't know anything about caring for a baby, then find someone who does who can teach you. Devote time to study and seek out counsel on being a mom or dad. Your child deserves your best. Even if as a child you didn't get someone else's best, this child shouldn't have to pay for other people's inadequacies. It is all the more reason for you to be to this child what you wish you would have had.

The third part is one that is often either forgotten or discarded, but it is really the most important. Trust God. When I finally saw this for what it was, it revolutionized my life. I am inadequate in myself as a son, a husband, and a father. I try very hard to be what I need to be in all of those roles, but in my own self and my own strength I fall short. Sometimes I have fallen miserably short. One day I finally realized that I would continue to fall short because I don't have all the answers, and I don't have all the angles covered. There are times I am in the dark, feeling the walls, trying to find my way. As I've learned to trust God, I've watched Him make up for my inadequacies in the lives of my children. They are His children first, and He wants what is best for them. I remembered what the Apostle Paul learned and spoke of in 2 Corinthians 12:9:

> *"My grace is sufficient for you, for My strength is **made perfect in** weakness."* (Emphasis mine.)

In my weakness His strength enters and does what I am unable to do. When Paul received this explanation, he had been dealing with a very trying situation that he had asked God to take him out of. God didn't remove him from the situation, but instead gave him grace to handle it.

When I was growing up, I used to hear people talk about the grace of God. It was a wonderful thing, this grace they talked about. It had gotten people through the loss of a loved one, broken relationships, illness, and financial hardships. The grace of God was what sustained them through their tough times.

As I grew into my teenage years, I continued to hear about this grace that God gave, and while I knew it was something special in the lives of many I knew, it seemed elusive to me. I studied it in my Bible and it was clearly there, but in life I really couldn't quantify it in a way that made it real to me. I knew that God's grace was active in my life, but I couldn't put my finger on how I could define it for myself.

What a Root Canal Taught Me about God's Grace

Let me give you a bit of back story to put this pivotal episode in my life in perspective. As a young boy I was found to have severe allergies. It seemed to me that I was allergic to more things than I was not allergic to. One of those allergies was to milk.

I couldn't drink milk, and instead I had to take calcium pills. Chalky, yucky, calcium pills. No milk. No real ice cream. Not fun for a seven year old.

A by-product of my condition was that the lack of calcium caused my teeth not to develop a proper layer of enamel on them. This made my teeth very susceptible to cavities. Brush as I may, the cavity creeps were successful in performing their mantra of "We make holes in teeth" in my mouth.

My first dentist was an older gentleman who was also my father's dentist. He was a gruff fellow who still wore the headband with the mirror attached, and he smelled of cigar smoke. I always found it interesting that I would get a lecture from him about my unhealthy penchant for Jolly Ranchers and Tootsie Pops, yet he obviously smoked. I had the presence of mind never to bring up that perceived disparity to him while I was in his dentist chair. Even at seven I was practicing some portion of wisdom and self-preservation.

On one visit a cavity was found that would require a filling. Not to worry, he advised that he could take care of that while my dad waited in the reception room. As my dad sat in that front room reading a magazine, my dentist proceeded to probe, drill, and fill. What he had neglected to do was give me a shot of Novocain or any other numbing agent first. You're reading this right, as a seven year old I got my first filling 'au naturel'. I felt the whole thing, smelled the whole thing, and made lots of noise through the whole thing. Needless to say, from that moment forward I had a distrust for dentists and a severe aversion to getting in the dental chair.

Over the years necessity has put me into that chair many times, with each experience better than that first one, but still dreaded nonetheless. In my early thirties I got the news that I had hoped never to hear—I was in need of a root canal. It wasn't something I could ignore, as it would soon be an abscess. Reluctantly I agreed, and the appointment was made.

The day came to go see the dentist, and my wife did her best to encourage me as I headed to my date with pain. As I arrived, I was taken to one of the back rooms where they seated me and prepped me for the procedure. I laid back in the chair and watched as the dentist came in. He was an older gentleman who assured me not to be concerned, because he had been doing the procedure for thirty years and would take good care of me. "Would you like something to take the edge off?" he asked me. "Yes, please," I replied. I was thinking, "Give me whatever you can to get me through this!"

As I lay there looking up, I silently started to pray. I was very nervous and anticipated a lot of discomfort and pain. It was then that I heard a voice on the inside of me say something that surprised me . . .

"There's a grace available for this."

I thought, "A grace available for this root canal? Huh?"

"Yes, a grace is available for this. You only need to access it."

I laid there dumbfounded. Grace was available to help me get through this root canal. I knew I needed help, and God had made grace available to me right then, right there. I laid there and said, "Lord, I take the grace You've made available for me in this time, and I thank You for it."

The dentist soon came back in and performed the procedure. I had no apprehension, no fear, and, to my surprise, there had been little given to me to mellow me out. I left the office with a completed root canal and went home for the day. I only had to take two Tylenol afterwards to handle the pain. I had made it through a seemingly terrible event with little adverse effects. More importantly, grace was no longer some wispy thing that floated in the air and might rest on you from time to time. Grace had become personal to me. God knew what I would be going through on that day and had made His grace available to me to get me through it.

As we discuss God's grace, I am aware that there are different facets and discussions regarding the subject. In the context of our discussion, we are addressing God's personal involvement to reach into our lives and to help us in areas where we are inadequate in our own strength. God's grace is made available to you and me by His love for us and His desire to be intimately involved in our lives. You could define this grace as *God's presence and power made available to us in a situation on our behalf to do what we are unable to do on our own.* The beauty of this is that it isn't some random occurrence in our lives.

There is no wheel of chance that is spinning up in heaven that might land on your name, and you get the pleasure of God's grace for that day. God's grace is available to you and me because of this; He has looked down the entirety of our lives and has seen each situation we will face. In doing this, He has also deposited His grace—*His presence and power made available to us in a situation on our behalf to do what we are unable to do on our own*—in those situations so that it is available to us to help us handle the situation and come out on the other side stronger. It's personal to you and me.

> *God's grace is made available to you and me by His love for us and His desire to be intimately involved in our lives.*

He knew that I would lose my mother when I was twelve years old, and He made His grace available to me throughout the following years to help me deal with the loss and her absence. He knew that I would be a single dad who was struggling to make sense of things, and He made His grace available to me to guide me and teach me. He knew I would be working for a company that would go bankrupt (Thanks, World.com), and His grace was available to preserve my position through seven layoffs and provide me with a telecommunications job in my same city when, supposedly, there weren't any available. He knew that at forty-three I would be diagnosed with latter stage cancer, and His grace was there to see me and my family through the treatment, financial strain, and the miraculous healing I received. There was many a day when I would lay in my bed during those hard days, weak and tired, and I would think about that day in the chair waiting to begin that root canal. I would remember that there was a grace that He had set aside for me, and I would draw on that grace to get me through the day.

Yes, His grace was and is personal to me. It's not a wisp that floats by and seeps through your fingers. It's His indelible touch, the hand on your shoulder, the pat on your back that lets you know you're not alone. This grace is sufficient. Paul discovered that. I discovered it. So can you.

It was this same grace that Joseph relied upon as he took Mary as his wife, Jesus as his son, and an uncharted course in the next years of his life. He faced so many situations that were precarious. Twists and turns? Joseph faced huge ones. He had no way that he could handle them in his own strength. How did he handle them? As we've seen earlier, he was open to God and relied on God. In situations where his understanding ran out, he was open to God's leading and intervention. He trusted God to fill in the holes that he had. When Joseph responded to the angel's instructions and took Mary as his wife, he did the best he could in the situation, but he didn't have all the answers. Just as he trusted God when he was obedient to the instructions, he trusted God to be in the details he was unaware of or unable to handle on his own.

Joseph was about to take Mary in her late stage of pregnancy from Nazareth to Bethlehem to comply with the census.

Were bandits possible along the way? Yes.

Was Mary's going into early labor possible? Yes.

Was bad weather possible? Yes.

What about the chance that there would be no comfortable place for Mary once they arrived in Bethlehem? It was a distinct possibility.

These were very important considerations Joseph had to deal with, and each was beyond his control.

Taking it into the realm of parenthood for Joseph, how does one go about parenting a child who is born without a sinful nature? How do you relate to a five year old that you realize is the Messiah, your Savior? What about the new dynamics of having other children in the family? This would be like going through the maze blindfolded and being forced to wear oven mitts. This was totally uncharted territory. In fact, Joseph will be the only man *ever* to face many of these unique situations. How did he do it? He relied on God's grace, *God's presence and power made available to him in a situation on his behalf to do what he was unable to do on his own.* Whether it was God giving him wisdom and insight in how to deal with a situation or God moving in the life of Jesus or one of the other children to do for and be to them what Joseph was unable to, God's grace was there to meet the need. I'm so thankful God gets personal with each of us if we will allow Him to.

As we've talked about fumbling around as we try our best to parent, it's only fitting that I give an example of how by His grace God stepped in one afternoon to teach me a better way to parent and to be a better man. In a few moments He changed my perceptions of many things and took me to a better, higher place in understanding of how to be a better father, how to understand Him better, and how to appreciate the father with whom He had blessed me. While God is so definitely invested in the small details of who we are, He also delights in opening our eyes to the bigger picture of who He is and what His ways are. I am so thankful for His love and patience, and how He worked with me that day to teach me and to take me deeper into both.

God's Affirming Approach to Growing You and Me

As I was growing up, I often heard sermons on God's discipline and His judgment. It was all right there in the Bible for everyone to see. I can still remember thinking as a child that in the Old Testament if your nationality ended in "ite," the chances were high that you were going to be judged and annihilated at some point. Over the years I came to understand that God's judgments on those people in the Old Testament were consequences that were brought on them by an unrepentant attitude toward Him and His purposes. I came to understand He wasn't doing covert surveillance on my life to catch me doing something wrong and punish me accordingly. He was watching over me to help guide me into right thinking and right actions.

As I grew in my relationship with God and my knowledge of the Bible, I learned that God disciplines those He loves, and that discipline is a proof of our belonging to Him. His discipline and correction in my life were a part of His active participation in molding me into the person He had created me to be. He was taking a vested interest in what I was to become, not merely passing judgment on what I had done.

After becoming a parent, I began to see things with a greater perspective. I no longer happily rested in the knowledge alone that God loved me and would correct me from time to time because of it. I came to understand the motivation behind that discipline. I had become *motivated* by the actions of my young son to instruct him in ways to keep him safe, keep him happy, and to keep Dad pleased with him. It wasn't just that I loved him and that's why I told him "NO" when he reached out toward the hot stove. My unending affections toward him were not the only reason I had the long discussion with my two year old about why we don't put army men down the toilet. That love for him was the basis of those conversations, but there was much more depth behind them than that.

What I came to understand is that my desire to prepare him to live safely and productively was very important. I not only wanted him to be safe, but I also wanted him to enjoy life and all that God had planned for him. I also wanted us to be able to live in harmony together, and that would require him following my rules. That discipline that I admittedly muddled my way through on different occasions had a purpose of instilling things in my son that I hoped would serve him well in life.

I can remember a specific day when he was about nine years of age and had been disobedient. I'd given him multiple chances to correct his behavior, but he hadn't acted on those chances. It had become time for discipline in the Clark home and Chief Justice Dad was prepared to deliver it and the previously detailed and prescribed punishment. As we walked back to his room to have our discussion, I was not pleased with his defiance, his lack of respect, or his attitude in general. I remember thinking that if he didn't change his tune quickly, it was not going to go well for him.

As we went into his room and closed the door behind us, I looked into his teary eyes and thought to myself, "I'm doing this for your own good." And I was in a way. I was trying to teach him not to be disobedient. In all honesty, as he began to squirm and try to talk his way out of his punishment, I began to get frustrated with him, and I could feel myself beginning to become angry. As he turned around for his swats, I heard the Holy Spirit speak to me on the inside, "Will you teach him to mind you, or teach him to correct himself like I do you?" It was as if time stood still. Here I was in the middle of disciplining my son, and the Holy Spirit had stepped in to discipline me. And I understood it as such. He hadn't accused me of something, hadn't browbeaten me, berated me, or tried to make me feel worthless. He had asked me a simple, insightful question to make me see something bigger. He had brought perspective to me and challenged me. He had introduced a new motivation in the ways I disciplined my son.

That day changed my life. I understood what God was trying to teach me. I turned my son back around and instead of reciting to him what he had done wrong and why he was being punished, I did a novel thing—I began to teach him about using self-control, making right decisions, and correcting yourself before someone else is forced to do it for you. That's how God is with us. He works to show us the right ways and to teach us to judge ourselves. I understood that was to be my goal as a parent as well. Discipline was not just about correcting bad behavior; it was about *discipling* our kids to walk before and with God. To this day my kids know my mantra at the first signs of things getting out of hand . . . "Do you want to correct yourself, or shall Mom and I have to do it for you? It's your choice."

After we had a good talk, I did give him one swat to follow through with the lingering consequences of the day's actions. There was no crying, no squirming. He understood it was his consequence, and he took it accordingly. Dad was very soft armed that day on that swat, and once it was done my son turned around and we hugged. What started out as an episode of Law and Order became a learning experience for us both and a time of bonding. My son got to see that I cared about *him* by the way I handled the situation. We spent the rest of the afternoon playing together and enjoying each other's company.

That time of correction was about helping my son learn to be a better boy, not about displaying my displeasure with his earlier behavior. It also served as a life lesson in how our Heavenly Father goes about disciplining us. No wrath, no malice, no need to make someone pay the price for His displeasure. All those things were placed on Jesus when He gave Himself on the cross for you and me.

When God comes to a place of discipline with us, His desire is to help us see the error of our ways so that we can make the needed adjustments ourselves. He is a Creator, not a destroyer. He thrives on building things up, not tearing them down. Throughout the Bible we see example after example of God patiently working with people to try to grow them to a new place of maturity in Him. Our Heavenly Father affirms His children, as He loves to pronounce blessing over them, to think wondrous thoughts about them, and to speak highly of them. The wrath and judgment that are found in the Bible are a result of those who chose not only to disregard God, but in many cases to thumb their noses at Him in defiance.

The Blessing of a Godly Father

I grew up in a home where punishment was an assured thing. Things weren't wishy-washy; they were cut and dried.

My dad was a man of his word, and what he said to us he kept. That included his following through on whatever consequences he had warned us of should we misbehave. It was never heavy-handed, never out of anger. I seldom saw him get worked up about anything, and to this day I can't recall witnessing him lose his temper. If we crossed the line, we paid the consequences, and then everyone moved on.

With the punishment didn't come a verbal brow-beating. I was never drawn through a long history of my mistakes and told what a shameful child I was. Punishment wasn't an event that my dad used to vent his aggravation and frustration with me. It wasn't about him; it was about what he wanted me to become and not to become. He was definitely dealing with the here and now when he was spanking me for my actions, but he understood that he was hoping to mold my behavior for the future.

In my dad's disciplining, there wasn't a big production, a blow-up of yelling.

Instead what I got was "the look." It wasn't a contrived expression created solely for the effect it would have on me. It was just this natural face my father would make that conveyed his disappointment in what I had done. No anger, no disgust—just disappointment. It was almost unbearable. The spanking or the grounding were painful to my posterior or my social life, but what pained me the most was the thought that I had disappointed my dad, that I had let him down. I can honestly say that the thought of disappointing my dad was more a motivating factor of my making good decisions than the thought of the punishment was. The punishment was a given consequence, but disappointing my dad had a whole different level of ramifications that I did not want to experience. That look didn't convey to me that I was a failure. What it said to me was "Son, you're better than that." It was not that he thought lowly of me; instead it was that he thought highly of me, and I had missed that mark in that particular situation.

Much of this had to do with his approach to me. While I didn't see it for what it was then, I now realize that those talks we had during my teenage years were about teaching me to think and to evaluate my own actions instead of his merely reacting to what I had done. He wasn't patting me on the head telling me what a good boy I was. He was talking to me as a reasoning human being who needed guidance. He affirmed my ability to think and my need to think beyond myself. He let me know when I made good decisions and when he thought I made ones that weren't so good. In those times I was never made to feel stupid or a failure. His classic line was, "Well, son, I wouldn't have made that decision or done it that way." He would give his advice if asked, but he only offered it unsolicited when he saw me prepared to make a major mistake. His counsel was almost always right on the button, and I learned to value it greatly.

God is the same way with us. He is always willing to advise us if asked but won't force Himself upon us. If we are listening for His voice, He will attempt to head us away from bad situations because He loves us. One thing we can be sure of is that His advice is always right. His ways with us are gentle, yet firm. He is controlled, methodical, and constructive. His intent in correction is to correct our thinking and in turn correct our behavior.

In dealing with us God will always be honest in His assessment of our attitudes and behaviors. He will let us know in what areas we are making progress and in those in which we are lacking. He lovingly takes the time to counsel us, mold us, and sustain us as we strive to become more in the image of Jesus—growing in His character and moving forward to fulfill what we were created for. He takes up where we are inadequate and adds His more than adequate self to the equation. We then become better than who we could be in our own strength. Better parents. Better sons and daughters. Better husbands and wives.

I'm so thankful for the grace of God in my life. That grace has been shown to me in so many different ways, and it is His grace that carries me through life's twists and turns. Just as in that little bedroom those years ago, God's grace has continued to correct my thinking and helped me be a better dad. It's helped me be a better husband and a better son. Even now He continues to work in me to mold me to become more like Him. It's an ongoing process, but I am learning and growing.

Major on the Majors

There are so many things we need to teach our children as we raise them. Some are very fundamental—how to walk, how to talk, how to eat with utensils, and the all-important how to use the big person potty. Then the next portions come along that are more protective in nature—hot things burn, sharp things cut, do not stick things in the electrical socket, and do not play in the toilet.

Relational teaching also happens as we teach our children to say "Please" and "Thank You." We instruct them to play with others, to share with others, and, important in the evolution of these interactions—not to hit others.

The instruction of our children is an ongoing process that never truly stops. What changes over time is that our role in instruction evolves, too. Even with my kids in their twenties, I've found myself reaching out to find the maze wall from time to time. I've found it often has had more to do with the way my role to them has changed than it does with the actual guidance required. I find myself no longer being the authority figure they needed when they were younger. They are now making their own decisions and are seeking my counsel, not necessarily my permission. I have to admit I've struggled with the change from time to time, but I've grown into things as I've allowed God to show me how to adjust. Other than either their or my departing this earth, I find myself in a situation from which I won't be removed, much like Paul found himself.

Thankfully, God saw ahead and knew I'd be facing this. He knew I would need help navigating this new season of my life. His grace was there when I asked for it, and it has made a difference.

As you read this, please know that what I am explaining isn't reserved for a select few. God shows no favoritism (Ephesians 6:9, Romans 2:11, Luke 20:21), and He willingly responds to those who seek Him (Proverbs 8:17, Hebrews 11:6, Psalm 9:10, Psalm 34:10).

When Joseph faced the daunting task of taking Mary and her child into his life and home, he had few answers about either his immediate future or the coming years. He chose to trust God, and God met him where he was and led him to the places and situations God had for him in each season of his life. God will do the same for you and me as we place our trust in Him and ask for His help.

Chapter 7

⌒⟶⟶⟶

WHAT THE BIBLE SAYS ABOUT GOD'S INVOLVEMENT IN OUR LIVES

Many years ago I wondered just how involved God wanted to be in my life. I knew that He loved me so much that He sent His Son Jesus to come and die in my place for my sins, but did the everyday events of my life interest Him enough to become involved with them at their lowest level? Did He care about what I thought or how I felt on any given day, or had He dealt with my sin problem and now it was up to me to try to stay out of trouble until I died? I knew I was going to heaven, but was I passing the time and trying to be good, or was there more to it? I really wasn't sure.

As I got older, studied my Bible, and saw more of life, I came to the conclusion that life was going to be a bumpy ride if God had done His part and had left me to figure out the rest on my own. Every day brings its own triumphs and challenges.

As I looked to the Bible for answers, I began to understand that God desired to be involved in my life as much as I would allow Him to be. He wasn't interested in being just a "Get Out of Hell" card. He was interested in being my Heavenly *Father*, not just my sponsor into eternity. He was there from my beginning and will be with me, period. That was a huge relief to me.

The beauty of this is that I don't have some exclusive arrangement with God that isn't available to the general public. God isn't a respecter of persons.

As I've laid out in the previous chapters, God wants to be intimately involved in your life. He's not watching over you like a parole officer. He wants to watch over you and help you as a loving parent would.

Think about that for a second. The God of Creation wants to watch over you as a loving parent—a parent who is interested in the highs and lows of your life, and He's not interested in this for mere informational purposes; He wants to be there to lend a helping hand and be a shoulder to cry on.

In 1 Peter 5:6-7 we read the following:

"Therefore humble yourselves under the mighty hand of God, that He may exalt you in due time, casting all your care upon Him, for He cares for you."

As a loving parent, He's willing to have you casting all your care on Him, for He cares for you. To say it another way—God cares for you, and invites you to take the cares and worries that burden you and cast them onto Him. It's not that you cast your cares on Him and then He decides to care about you. He begins by caring about you so much that He desires you to cast those cares on Him in order to lighten your load. Does God care about the details of your life? The answer is yes. Those details are your *cares*.

So how detailed is God about you and me? Jesus talked of this in Matthew 10:29-30:

> *Are not two sparrows sold for a copper coin? And not one of them falls to the ground apart from your Father's will.*
>
> *But **the very hairs of your head are all numbered.***
> (Emphasis mine.)

The first time I saw that scripture it amazed me. The very hairs on my head are numbered. He pays attention to them. God has taken a full inventory of me. At over fifty years of age, I've noticed that my hair inventory has been slowly reducing in number. Each time one ends up in my comb, I envision some tracking sign up in heaven with my name on it, and the number of my counted hairs on it reducing by one. Although it still bugs me, I've decided as long as it is being tabulated by simple subtraction and not division I can live with it.

Now with this amazing detailed view of you and me, God goes further. He hasn't merely been keeping an inventory of us, He has plans for you and me as well. We are told of this in Jeremiah 29:11:

> *For I know the thoughts that I think toward you, says the LORD, thoughts of peace and not of evil, to give you a future and a hope.*

God is thinking of you and me, and the thoughts He has for us are of peace and not evil. Think about that. As God keeps track of the minute details of your being, He is thinking of you, and the thoughts He thinks *toward* you are of peace, not evil. Those thoughts He has *toward* you are His intentions and His desires for you. He *desires* peace for you, not evil. He desires that peace for you because He also desires that you have a future and a hope. He wants to bring peace into your life so that you can have hope for your future, a future He has planned for you.

Another rendering of the verse that I like, taken from the United Bible Societies' Old Testament Handbook Series, puts it this way:

> *"I will give you the kind of life where you can know that good things will happen to you in the future."*

His thoughts and intention for you and me are for us to have the kind of life where we can know good things will happen to us in the future. The only way we will have that kind of life is with His being involved. Since He wants this for us, He will stay engaged in our lives to help us realize His desire for us.

When my mom passed away, I had several people come to me and pledge to be there for me, to take me places she had wanted to take me, to watch over me, and to be a listening ear and a shoulder to cry on when needed. They all meant well. Their desire was to comfort me and give me hope that the coming weeks and years would have meaning, and that those times wouldn't be lonely. It didn't take long before the passage of time and the busyness of life had those people become distant and detached from my daily life. I don't fault them, as I'm sure I have unknowingly done the same thing before.

I could have felt alone, but God had blessed me with a wonderful Dad and great friends. Most of all, He was with me. During those teen years He became real to me, a source of comfort and of hope. It's at this time that I came to realize that He was ready, willing, and able to be involved in my life as much I would allow Him to be. He wasn't just well meaning. He didn't become too busy to be with me. God was there to listen to me vent my frustrations, my hurts, my insecurities, and my requests for help. Big or small, He listened. He will listen, and He gives grace to those who seek Him.

We see this in James 4:6 NIV:

"God opposes the proud but gives grace to the humble."

The proud would be those who believe they have no need for God, that they are sufficient in themselves. The humble person is one who recognizes that he is not sufficient in himself to overcome all of life's challenges, and he needs help.

That person looks to God as the answer to his weakness, and God's grace is made available to him or her. Even deeper, that person realizes that God's intentions are for a future filled with hope, and he responds to God as his basis for that hope. God responds in kind.

He gives grace. Do you remember the definition we used in the last chapter for this grace we're talking about? *God's power and presence made available to us in a situation on our behalf to do what we are unable to do on our own.* His power and presence. **Presence.** He is present and His power is made available. He's not far off; He is present. That is what I would call being involved.

But God didn't become involved in our lives as we became teens or grew into adulthood. It's not as if He waited to see how we were turning out before He decided at what level He wanted to interact with you or me. He has been involved with us from the beginning.

We can track this back in the scripture to even before our birth. In Psalm 71:5-6 NLT, David speaks of God being with him from birth:

> *"O Lord, you alone are my hope. I've trusted you, O Lord, from childhood.*
>
> *Yes, **you have been with me from birth; from my mother's womb you have cared for me.**"* (Emphasis mine.)

David goes even further with his description in Psalm 139:13-18:

> *You made all the delicate, inner parts of my body and knit me together in my mother's womb.*
>
> *Thank you for making me so wonderfully complex! Your workmanship is marvelous—how well I know it.*
>
> *You watched me as I was being formed in utter seclusion, as I was woven together in the dark of the womb.*
>
> *You saw me before I was born. Every day of my life was recorded in your book.*
>
> *Every moment was laid out before a single day had passed.*
>
> *How precious are your thoughts about me, O God.*
>
> *They cannot be numbered!*
>
> *I can't even count them; they outnumber the grains of sand! . . .*

In this passage David goes into great detail to speak of how intricately God was involved in his formation from the moment of conception. In His description God isn't sitting on a throne in some distant place, observing with a passing interest. David says in verse 13:

> *"You made all the delicate, inner parts of my body and knit me together in my mother's womb."*

God made the delicate parts of the body and knit them together in the mother's womb. God *made* and *knit*. Those words describe a hands-on approach to David's life in the most formative stages of his existence. Beyond that, he goes on to say in verse 16:

> *You saw me before I was born. Every day of my life was recorded in your book.*
>
> *Every moment was laid out before a single day had passed.*

Before he was born, God saw him, and every day of his life was known and recorded before a single day had passed. God in His omniscience was aware of every moment of every day that David would live. There would be good days; there would be bad days. There would be horrible days. David would make good choices, and he would make inexcusable choices. There would be days where his own actions would have drastic effects, and there would be days where the actions of others would have devastating effects on his own life. God saw them all. He then goes on to say in verses 17 and 18:

> *How precious are your thoughts about me, O God. They cannot be numbered!*
>
> *I can't even count them; they outnumber the grains of sand!*

Read that a few times and let it sink in. The thoughts God had for David couldn't be numbered. The thoughts He has for you and me outnumber the grains of sand. The God of the universe moved to form you in your mother's womb and has had innumerable thoughts about you. That is mind-boggling. Does that make you wonder why He is this way about you?

You're Captivating to God

I didn't start out as the by-product of a couple's romantic interlude, and neither did you. Those are just the circumstances of how we got to this place we now call home.

This really all started somewhere in times past. There was a point in time where God had a thought that He pondered upon. That thought became a point of interest with Him so much that He pondered on it and the thought developed into an idea. As God thought on that idea, He began to see many facets to it that inspired Him. This idea was something that drew in His interest to the point that He became captivated with its possibilities. It was no longer enough to merely entertain the idea. This idea was so captivating to God that He desired for it to have a form, a representation that He could freely interact with and enjoy. As He lovingly formed the shell that would encase His captivating idea, it was so pleasing to Him that He even was willing to breathe His own breath into it to bring it to its own conscious state. He so desired to interact with it, to relate to it, and to see it fulfill all that He had envisioned it to accomplish.

As He formulated all that this idea would encompass, He then looked down the corridors of time to find the place that He would most need this captivating thought to become live and active in. This thought that had become an idea also had a plan and a destiny in the mind of God, and He would place it at the exact time and place He knew it would have the desired impact. He then looked through every moment of every day that it would exist, and He lovingly placed His grace in those areas where they would be needed. He carefully moved from event to event and appointed His presence and its accompanying power to be ready for use in each needed situation. Then He stepped back and reached His own hand into the appointed time for this captivating idea to come into the realm of man, where He breathed His own breath into the small form and watched it grow until it came forth . . .

That thought that became a captivating idea in the mind of God, that idea that had excited Him so much He had to bring it into its own form that He could interact with and relate to, was born. **It was you.** Those innumerable thoughts that God had for you began when He first thought of you, pondered about you, became enthralled with you, planned you, provided His grace for you, and breathed His life into you. You aren't an afterthought. The thought of you *captivated* God, and He acted to bring you to a place where He could interact and relate to you. That feeling He had about you never passed.

You *still* captivate God.

With this in mind, as we read Psalm 8:3-4 NLT, we can now answer the question it poses:

When I look at the night sky and see the work of your fingers—the moon and the stars you set in place— what are mere mortals that you should think about them, human beings that you should care for them?

What are people that He should think about them, that He should care for them?

We are each unique, treasured ideas that captivated God to the point of creating us so that He could interact with us. Each captivating idea is so precious to God. He thinks of it and cares for it. He thinks of you and me and cares for us.

The thought of you captivated God, and He acted to bring you to a place where He could interact and relate to you.

The scriptures are very clear that God is intricately involved in who we are before, during, and after we are physically formed. In Isaiah 44:2 we find God saying,

"Thus says the LORD who made you and formed you from the womb. . . ." Notice, He says who made you AND formed you in the womb. Psalm 139 paints a beautiful picture of God's detailed involvement in all the facets of who we are, from His initial creative thoughts of us through our conception and forming in our mother's womb, to the purpose He gave us to fulfill in our lives. God didn't mass produce your model and

place them on the earth. You are a unique creation of God Almighty. Never doubt it. Never forget it.

CHOICES

So inevitably the question is going to come up: "If God is so captivated with me that He thinks of me constantly and wants to be involved in my life, why has my life been such a mess?"

It's a fair question. I'll be honest with you—I don't have an answer to address each situation you've faced in your life. I don't have an answer for every situation I've faced in my life. Why did I lose my mom in a car wreck? Why did I have cancer? I could make quite a list on my own. I can tell you the one answer I've been able to rely on is trusting in that same attention that God has for me, that He sees what I'm dealing with and is moved with compassion to come alongside of me and help me get through it.

There are so many different factors that enter into why and how things happen in life. In the context of this book we've been talking about what God looked for in the man who would be the earthly father to His Son. When God was surveying mankind to find the man most suitable to fill this role, He was looking at each man with the understanding that each had a free will. With that free will he could come to his own conclusions, make his own decisions, and pursue his own actions. People were going to be making choices of their own accord. Sure, they could be influenced in different ways as they made their choices, but those choices were theirs to make.

When God chose to create you and me, He did so in a way that would be most satisfying to Him. He gave us the right to choose. To have created something that had no choice but to worship Him would have been hollow praise. You've probably been in a situation before where either people said nice things about you because they really didn't have much choice, or you had to give those compliments (aka lip service) to someone else. It feels all wrong and uncomfortable, like wearing wet socks. It amounts to little more than a verbal golf clap. There is no satisfaction in it.

God feels the same way. To compel someone to love you isn't love, it's coercion and self-indulgence. For someone to choose to love you, that is fulfillment. To be chosen makes us feel special and wanted. That is what you and I desire, and it has been God's desire as well. When we willingly choose to love Him and follow after Him, it provides fulfillment to Him. He made you and me with the ability to choose so that the relationship He can share with us is one that can grow in depth over time. Remember the phrase from Psalm 8:4 NLT?

"What are mere mortals that you should think about them, mere human beings that you should care for them?"

He cares for us and desires that we would care for Him. It's this same care that motivated Him when searching for the man who would ultimately be Joseph. The man that God chose would be making constant choices that would impact the life of His Son.

He would inspect the man's thought processes, his values, his character—everything that would influence the choices that he would make.

Beyond that, He would also be evaluating the man on how he would be able to teach His Son about choices. He would have to teach Jesus on what to base His choices, how to make them, and how to live with the outcomes of the choices. The same would apply to Mary, as God would have searched the hearts and minds of both of Jesus' earthly parents to insure that their character was a reflection of His and their regard for His Word and His ways was the guiding factor in their decision-making.

As parents we bear the same responsibility before God, to become in tune and in alignment with His Word and His ways as we live our lives and raise our children. Our responsibility in God's eyes is not just to raise our children to adulthood, but just as it was to Joseph and Mary, to raise them as God would have us raise them.

BAD CHOICES AREN'T THE END

In giving us this ability to make our own choices, God left Himself open to the possibility that we would choose not to have a relationship with Him. We could make choices that would go against Him. In the face of this, He willingly gave you and me the ability to choose because He saw the possibility of having this relationship with us was worth the risk. He was willing to take that chance in order to relate with that captivating idea that had enthralled Him. It led Him to bring that idea of having someone with whom to interact into existence.

This freedom to make our own choices, or "free will," comes with its own set of variables. When we make a choice, it sets situations and circumstances into motion. As a husband, my choices affect my wife. As a father, my choices affect my children and our family. As a boss, my decisions affect those who are underneath me. Every day there are consequences to the choices you and I make. Some we face personally, while others impact those around us.

In my upbringing I was fortunate to have loving parents who made their choices with my best interests in mind. Many people haven't had that same experience. You may be reading this book and much of what has been discussed sounds good, but it is far from what you've experienced in life. Your parents may have been distant; they may have been abusive. You may have not grown up with any parents. The choices that others in your life have made have had a major impact on your life. Again the question comes . . .

"If God's so captivated with me that He thinks of me constantly and wants to be involved in my life, why has my life been such a mess?"

Some of it may have to do with the choices others in your life have made, and the ways their choices have affected you. Other issues may be because of the choices you have made. This is what we all face, what we all deal with in one form or another. But there is hope!

Remember our beginning passage from this chapter?

First Peter 5:6-7 states:

Therefore humble yourselves under the mighty hand of God, that He may exalt you in due time, casting all your care upon Him, for He cares for you.

Those cares are the results of choices that have been made. Some may be a result of what your parents chose to do. Some may be a result of what a family member or friend chose to do. Many will be as a result of choices we have made for ourselves.

Those choices bring outcomes which can be favorable or unfavorable. It's those resulting outcomes that become the cares that you and I carry along. It is those cares that God tells us to cast or lay over onto Him, because He cares for us. His presence and power, the grace that comes alongside us to lighten our burden and help us through what we are facing, takes the weight and provides the relief.

Don't allow yourself and your life to be defined by your or other people's bad choices. Allow God to be involved with you in your life. He desires to come alongside you and walk out your trials with you.

In Isaiah 61:3 NLT we see a picture of this:

To all who mourn in Israel, he will give a crown of beauty for ashes, a joyous blessing instead of mourning, festive praise instead of despair.

In their righteousness, they will be like great oaks that the Lord has planted for his own glory.

God gives beauty for ashes, blessing instead of mourning, and praise instead of despair.

I've been in situations that have seemed bleak. It seemed as if the things I had worked so hard to make successful had remained for a season, but had begun to come unraveled; and what I had thought would be a large part of my future was soon a virtual pile of rubble all around me. I wasn't going to give up, but things looked pretty bad. I felt the weight of those cares and worries begin to push down on my head, my shoulders, and my heart.

Those many years ago when I sat in my bedroom that night with the weight of being a single dad beginning to settle in, I did the wisest thing that could be done. I reached out to God, the God who was captivated with me. The God whose thoughts of me were of a future and a hope. The God who had told me in 1 Peter, chapter 5, to roll my cares and worries over on Him, because He cares for me.

Although I didn't understand it at the time, when I reached out to Him for His answers to my situation, His grace was there. His grace was there to answer my questions, guide me, and meet my needs. The answer He gave me in Joseph, the earthly father He had chosen for His Son, gave me a picture of the traits in my life that He wanted me to develop. I've come to realize over the years it also did something else so very precious for me—it allowed me to learn at a more personal level what God's character was and what His care toward me really encompassed. What He was showing me was that as Joseph sought to live a life that was pleasing to God, a life that was honorable in God's eyes, he was also an example of the kind of man God was looking for.

Joseph faced an uncertain life with a trust in God to care for him. It shaped his decisions and became his anchor through so many uncertain times. The events in the first two chapters of Matthew and Luke point to a man who understood that what God asked of him would also include God's grace to get him through. He would have cares and concerns, but God would be there to answer them. There was no formula on how God would move—only that He would do what He said He would do and be who He said He would be.

I want to encourage you that He is available to you just as He was for Joseph and has been for me so many times. His greatest desire is to interact with you, to relate to you on a personal level, and to be intimately involved in your life. His involvement isn't something you have to beg for. It's there for the asking.

Chapter 8

෴

WHERE THE RUBBER MEETS THE ROAD

In this book we've taken a look at Joseph and his story from several different angles:

- We have viewed how God looked upon him as He sought a man to be His Son's earthly father.

- We've looked into the events that Joseph dealt with as he came to find his betrothed pregnant with a child that was not his and how his following decisions and actions impacted his life.

- We've looked at the man and woman that God chose to be the earthly parents to His Son and the type of relationship they would have had with each other and the family they built together.

- We've defined the fruit of the Spirit, or character traits of God, from Galatians, chapter 5, and then illustrated each of them in Joseph's actions towards Mary and their situation.

- We've looked at the challenges of parenthood and how God's help is available to us to be the parents He desires us to be.

- We've looked at what the Bible has to say about God's desire for involvement in our lives.

It's been my intention to open up the life of Joseph in a way that takes him from being a brief but necessary side note in the life of Jesus and scripture and expand what we know of him. Doing so opens the curtains to show God's ways and to illustrate the importance that God gave to Joseph's role. This hasn't been intended to be an apology for Joseph, but rather a study in what God looked for in the earthly father for His Son and what He looks for us to be as parents to our children.

When I asked that question those many years ago regarding what I needed to be in order to be the father God intended me to be for my son, I understood I would not become that person overnight. I still haven't measured up to that person now. I still make mistakes from time to time, but I've had a blueprint to assess myself by over the years to help me see where I needed to improve. It's also helped me to help others when they've come to me with questions regarding raising their own children.

I don't have the market cornered on good parenting. I don't have a one-size-fits- all approach to recommend or a

12-step program to endorse. Life is full of twists and turns. How you end up with your kids is often one of those sudden twists. My wife and I have been there ourselves with a surprise we hadn't expected.

What do you do? I can tell you what we did; we did what Mary and Joseph did. We decided to go to God, explain to Him our dilemma, and ask Him for guidance and help. I can also tell you that things didn't work out overnight. We had lots of questions and concerns. She was a stay at home mom with two kids, one of whom was an eight- month-old baby girl. I was a student working full time in the evenings and barely making enough to make ends meet.

To our surprise we found we were going to have another baby. My wife saw her energy level finally returning after her last pregnancy and "Guess what!" Those little lines on that pregnancy test stick were not what she was hoping for at this time in her life. Just as things were beginning to settle in for her, she had the new concerns of how she would be able to manage two little ones and one in grade school while I was gone much of the week to school and work. She had every opportunity to wonder how we would be able to afford this new mouth to feed.

On my side of the coin, I was wondering how much more I would have to work to try to afford this new mouth to feed. Would I need to get another part-time job and be away from my family even more than I already was? We only had one car; how would I get back and forth to everywhere I needed to go?

I couldn't leave my wife and the kids at home with no way to get out. Should I drop out of school for now until things settled down? The spinning wheel of questions went on and on with no end in sight.

At some point over the next days and weeks, we did three important things. First, we breathed. Yes, breathed. We took a deep breath, collected ourselves from among those seemingly unending, swirling questions—and we breathed. There was no way we were going to have all the answers at that given moment, so we took the time to breathe and calm our racing minds. If you're going through anything like this in life, whether it be related to children, relationships, your job, or your finances—take time to breathe. Swirling winds never allow anything to settle, and swirling thoughts will never give you any peace or focus. Take a deep breath. When we saw Joseph faced with a swell of emotions after Mary told him she was pregnant with a child that wasn't his, at some point he took a deep breath. He collected himself and then moved forward. You can as well.

Secondly, we sought God on our own. That is to say, I went to God to list my concerns to Him, and she went to God to list her concerns. My wife is the most wonderful woman in the world as far as I am concerned (sorry, Mom), but there are questions I have in life that she can't answer, doesn't have the answer for, and wouldn't try to answer even if I pressed her on it. On the other hand, over the years I have proven that I don't always give her the best answers for what she needs, and she is a person who wants to and needs to hear from God for herself.

(Quick marriage tip—the quicker you realize that you are not the sole deliverer of wisdom and knowledge that your spouse has, the quicker you will be on your way to a better marriage. When God appears to you and writes His instructions for your spouse on tablets for you to deliver to her personally, then you *may* have reason to come to him or her as though you were Moses coming down from the mountain. And if that does occur, make sure you have the glory of God on your countenance as Moses did before you try to speak with that authority.)

When we each did this, God was able to answer our specific questions in ways that each of us needed in order to give us peace. The concerns didn't disappear, but they didn't grow to become worries that could consume us. What we received was reason to hope and strength from the One in whom we could place our hope. We cast our cares on God and trusted in Him to work things out for us because He cares for us. We didn't have our heads in the sand. We realized what we were facing. We also realized it was beyond us to solve everything on our own, and we trusted God to give us wisdom in areas where we were challenged.

Thirdly, we communicated. Granted, we'd only been married three years, so we were still learning how to communicate with each other. What we did do was try to share with each other as best we could how we each felt and what we could share from our own time of seeking God. This also allowed us to come together in unity, and helped us to trust God to help us in what we were facing. He was the answer to the concerns we had.

I would like to have had the revelation that God was that child's father first and foremost at this time in our lives, but I didn't. It would have helped me in those times when I was asking so many "How?" questions. Even through it all, God was so faithful to us in so many ways. It wasn't easy, and the road had more twists and turns, but that little girl made it safe and sound, and the many questions we were faced with all had answers that played out over time. God provided peace, resources, and guidance that saw us through.

That's exactly what we see in the account of Joseph and Mary in Matthew and Luke. There were so many twists and turns, far more dangerous and impactful than most of us will ever deal with. In each one, God was with them to see them through.

JOSEPH TOOK THE TIME TO BREATHE

After dealing with the shock of Mary's news, Joseph went into a mode of thought and introspection. We can see this by how he placed anger and retribution to the side and allowed himself to think with a cooler head as he moved toward a decision on how to handle the situation.

JOSEPH SOUGHT GOD OUT

While we don't have a specific verse that details the questions that Joseph struggled with in his own mind, and then went to God with, we see in Matthew 1:20 where the angel addresses issues specifically for Joseph. God would not have chosen a man to be the earthly father of His own Son who did not come to Him with his life's concerns. This man would be a man of humility whose reliance on God would be paramount to him fulfilling his call to be Jesus' earthly father. The angel brought answers from the throne of God to those questions Joseph had.

JOSEPH COMMUNICATED WITH MARY

In Matthew 1:24 we see that once Joseph had his angelic visitation in his dream, he proceeded to take Mary as his wife. For him to do so, he would have certainly had to address with her what had changed in the past hours about his belief in her story. He would have shared with her about his dream and about the angel's instructions. They would have become one in this calling and purpose and would rely on their continued communication as they raised Jesus from infancy to manhood.

God chose Joseph to be the earthly father to His Son because Joseph best fit the part of the man He desired. He saw the heart, the character, the internal strength, and the faith that would be required.

In Psalm 103:7 we read that God showed His actions to the children of Israel but to Moses He showed His ways. The children of Israel would not humble themselves to a place to know God intimately and were only able to witness God's wondrous acts on their behalf. Moses humbled himself in a manner that placed him where God could show him His ways—how He thought, how He perceived, His wisdom.

God wanted the same for His Son—to be raised not only by parents who knew of His acts, but by parents who acknowledged and walked in His ways. They would be people who would model this to their children. God saw this in Joseph and chose him.

Chapter 9

⚭

JOURNAL: PRIVATE THOUGHTS AND QUIET PRAYERS OF A CHOSEN FATHER

One of the greatest gifts my father gave me was the time he spent teaching me how to think for myself, not merely telling me what to think. As he did this, he always led me back to the Bible as the baseline for my decision making.

In the following pages you will find journal entries to illustrate what Joseph might have written as he recorded events in his life. They are in no way meant to be considered as an interpretation of anything more than what Joseph's journal or diary might have read. They have been constructed taking into account what we have discussed concerning what God looks for in a man's character, along with that man's corresponding thoughts and actions. The journal entries are meant to be a snapshot into events in Joseph's life, with his thoughts as an example of how we all can model ourselves to think more and act more with the character traits of God as our guide.

At the end of each journal entry you'll find thoughts for consideration, along with a short, related prayer. My hope is that these entries can provide you practical examples of how godly traits can influence our thoughts and the decisions we make.

PREPARING FOR A FUTURE

It won't be long and my life will change forever. In the coming weeks I will take Mary as my bride, and we will begin a new life together. There will be the two of us instead of one, and all of my decisions will need to reflect an understanding of this new reality.

There are many reasons why I have fallen in love with Mary. She is a lovely young woman, and I've become captivated by her. What has captivated me is who she is —gentle, compassionate, virtuous, and wise beyond her years. She has a way of making me laugh, and a gleam in her eye that reflects her wry sense of humor. I've never enjoyed being with someone as much as I do when I am with her.

I have some work to finish, and then I will go to visit Mary. She's been gone to visit her cousin Elizabeth for the last three months. Elizabeth had been unable to conceive a child for many years, and by a miracle of the Lord she conceived, even though she was up in years. I'm sure we'll spend time talking about the preparations for our wedding and for our home. For her gentleness, she can be assertive when she decides to be! I actually enjoy it at times—at least when I am not getting in trouble.

The future I see us having together is one that I've been looking forward to for many months. There comes a time in your life where you want to have someone with whom to share life. It's more than simply not wanting to be alone. I look at the physical home I'm preparing for Mary and me, and I see the concept in a way I never had before. I am building room for us to live in, to share our days and nights together. As I shape the wood and stone to fit and make a wall, a shelf, a bed, I am physically constructing where we will live. As Mary and I spend our days and years together as husband and wife, we'll be doing the same—although we'll be constructing a family and a life we share. Piece by piece, event by event, day by day.

As I've been thinking on this, I've come to realize that the care I take in preparing the wood and stone for this room needs to be the same type of care I take in building a life with Mary. I need to pay attention to what I do and what I say. Those things are important, just as how well I've measured and shaped the materials in this room are. These walls and furniture didn't just happen to fall into place; there was work and attention put into their preparation and placement. If I want to have a successful life with Mary, I will have to do the same. With that and my realization that I really don't understand women, I surely need God's help.

Thoughts to Consider

Success in life and in relationships takes dedication and work. Things don't magically fall into place time and time again, and it's unfair to the other party to blame them for life's struggles and disappointments when you sit back waiting for it all to work out without your participation or effort.

Realizing you don't have all the answers will help you to reach out to others for their help and guidance. It will also expand the possibilities for you to grow and be successful. Seeking God's wisdom for your life will provide the solid foundation you need to build your life upon.

Father, I come to You realizing that in my own wisdom and understanding I lack all that is necessary to live a life that is fulfilling to me and pleasing to You. Help me to see things as You do and to live my life in a way that represents those things that are near to Your heart. Help me to love others as You do and to treat them as I would want to be treated. Show me the way You would have me to go and how You would have me go about doing it. I trust You to be with me each day, knowing that Your promise to never leave me or forsake me is true. I thank You for Your love, Your guidance, and Your faithfulness. I ask this in the name of Your Son, Jesus. Amen.

BETRAYAL!

How things have changed in the last few hours. Earlier today I was an excited man going to visit my betrothed who has just returned from visiting her cousin. Now these few hours later I am a man whose betrothed has informed me that SHE is with child. I have never been with her in that way, so this child cannot be mine.

How could this happen? I was so sure that Mary was meant to be my wife, and that her faithfulness was without question. She had gone to visit her cousin Elizabeth, the wife of the priest Zacharias. Elizabeth had been unable to conceive for years, but an angel had appeared to her husband and announced that she would conceive a child. Shortly after the angel's appearance, Elizabeth did conceive, and Mary had gone to help Elizabeth during the latter part of her pregnancy. I didn't like that she would be gone for more than a month, but I understood that she was excited to be around this blessed occurrence, and her help would be invaluable to Elizabeth.

The circumstances around Elizabeth and Zacharias' conceiving of a child were nothing short of miraculous. Mary had shared the details with me, and we both had marveled at how the blessing of a child in old age that had been bestowed on Abraham and Sarah had now been bestowed on Elizabeth and Zacharias. And not just a miraculous conception, but an actual VISITATION from an angel. They are surely favored by God.

Now Mary has come back to me, my beautiful Mary. I sensed something was different, but I explained it away as being the excitement of having her back. As we sat there and she spoke to me of her visit, there was something in her eyes that told me there was more. I thought that maybe another miraculous event with Zacharias and Elizabeth had taken place. Mary had left before the birth of their child, so I thought there was some great new happening that had prompted her return. I was in no way prepared for what she told me next.

She seemed troubled yet excited all at the same time. I can still see her eyes looking deeply at me as she told me she was pregnant. I can still see the tears begin to well up in those eyes when she saw my reaction of dismay and pain. She said she was pregnant! Pregnant! All the hopes and preparations I had been making became as mists in the early morning when I heard her say those words.

I had dreamt of hearing those words, "Joseph, I am pregnant." Those words were supposed to be mine to savor as we celebrated the gift from God that was a symbol of our love for each other. Those words were for us to share in awe and thanksgiving as the God of our fathers had shown us favor in granting us a child. Those words I heard, but they were sour, devoid of any pleasure for me, and devastating to my soul. I expected them to be something other than the pain their circumstance has brought.

Anger and bitterness had risen up inside me, and I could easily have embraced them and passed them off as righteous indignation. Yet as quickly as they rose up in me, I pushed them away. In the midst of all the turmoil, I had the presence of mind not to give them root in me, for I knew they would only cause more pain for myself and others. After having a little time to reflect, I realized to give in to those feelings would be to rob myself of happiness and joy in the days to come. I've seen too many people who go through life harboring ill feelings for things that had taken place years before. That bitterness and resentment that initially had poisoned them over one area had spread into other areas of their lives and eventually made them miserables. They seemed to exist to replay past hurts and attempt to make the pain go away by spreading that pain to others. I have never been that way before, and I choose not to start now.

So what am I to do? At this point, how can I trust in Mary after this has happened? I do love her so very much, but how can I take her into my home as my wife, knowing that even before we had married she was unable to remain faithful to me? The consequences for her being with child out of wedlock are severe, and even more since she was betrothed. I do not want any harm to befall her—not even this child she is carrying.

I could serve her a bill of divorcement in a very discrete manner that would satisfy the law and then advise her father to send her away so that she faces no wrath from the community for her actions. That may be the best way to handle the situation.

I'm still very surprised at her explanation. As my mind was swirling with—How could this have happened? Who was this man she had betrayed me with? Did she not love me?—Mary told me that she had not been unfaithful to me. What? Not been unfaithful? How had she "faithfully" conceived a child with another man? Not just *known* another man—she'd CONCEIVED with another man! Yet in all of this she had not been unfaithful?

I was speechless and it was probably a good thing. She went on to tell me that she had been visited by the same angel that had visited Zacharias, and that this angel Gabriel had told her that she was highly favored by the Most High and had been chosen to be the mother of the Messiah. She went on to tell me that the angel told her that she would conceive this child by the Spirit of God, and not by any man. This all falls in line with the prophet's writings that the Messiah would be born of a virgin—but this was My Mary. We are not from Jerusalem, we are not of great means, and the prophet had written that the Messiah would be born in Bethlehem. We live in Nazareth.

I left upset and angry over the turn of events. Mary was crying—crying over the mess she was in, crying over hurting me, crying over the consequences of her actions; I'm not sure if it was one or all. Honestly I wasn't thinking clearly when

I left her father's home. What an explanation to top off the news that she was with child!

I know Mary, and she is not prone to exaggerations or wild stories. Maybe the recent events surrounding Elizabeth and Zacharias and her time with them provided her an idea she could use to make this dilemma one that is "no one's fault," and free her, the man she was with, and me from any responsibility. The problem with that line of thinking is that there are consequences no matter what the story used to explain how she is with child. And at some point later in life, this Messiah child will have to live up to His billing or even more ridicule will come upon Mary. None of it really makes any sense.

Sense. That's a word that I have little feel for right now. All I really know at this time is that:

1. I love Mary very much.

2. I am deeply hurt by her being with another man's child, and the unfaithfulness she has shown.

3. I do not want her or her child harmed, as I do not have it in my heart to seek retribution.

The best solution I see right now is the one where I put her away discretely by a bill of divorcement, and then her father sends her away to have the child in safety. Should word of what she has done come out, she and her child could be in grave danger.

It would be best for me to sleep on this all for tonight, and not make a hasty decision. I will be able to think clearly tomorrow and can move on from there. Ah, that the Lord would grant me peace and sleep this night . . .

Thoughts to Consider

Life can present us with surprises, sometimes in a most devastating way. These events can bring on a flood of thoughts and emotions that can be overwhelming. It takes time to handle the initial shock and to process the circumstances and events. It's vitally important that we don't let that flood of emotion carry us into making hasty decisions that haven't been thought out. The repercussions of those hasty decisions can sometimes lead to causing the situation to be worse than it originally was, or to creating new, devastating situations with far reaching consequences. Taking time to collect yourself and to get a handle on your thoughts and emotions can go a long way in helping you cope with what has happened and to make solid decisions that protect your future.

Prayer

Father, help me to keep control of my thoughts and feelings as I face this situation. I don't have the answers right now, but I know that this situation hasn't caught You off guard. You know the best way for me to face this and handle it. Please show me what I need to do during this time, and how You would have me do it. Give me strength and peace during this time as only You can. Thank You for being with me each step of the way. I ask these things in the name of Your Son, Jesus. Amen.

THE ANGEL IN MY DREAM

I went to bed last night still shaken by the news that Mary had told me about her being pregnant. I thought I'd come to a reasonable course of action but wanted to sleep on it and have a clearer head when I awoke. I had no idea how much things would change again—even in my sleep.

Sometime during the night I experienced an amazing thing. It seemed like a dream, but it was so real to me. An angel appeared to me and called me by name. He called me, "Joseph, son of David." To hear my name spoken and then the reference to King David caught me off guard. My ancestry traces back to him, but it isn't something that people give much credence to. I'm still amazed that the angel called me by name.

Then the angel directly addressed my situation with Mary. He actually validated the story she had told me and then included me in what is to happen next. I can still hear him saying, "Do not be afraid to take Mary as your wife." When he said that, it was as if all of those thoughts and concerns I had listed last night began to melt away, and they no longer were sources of mistrust or doubt. My being "afraid" to take Mary as my wife consisted of many things, but the angel's answer put them to rest. It's not as if he went down my list item by item. It's that when he said those words, I knew deep down I could trust those words to be true. I really can't describe it in detail yet, but there was a peace that came over me.

It is like when I was a child and the room would be dark. I would become afraid and call out for my father. I couldn't see him in the dark, but I would hear his voice saying to me, "Joseph, it is all right, I am right here." It was still dark, but that reassuring voice and those words made the fear go away.

I have little idea of what the future holds for me in the coming days, but I know that I will not be afraid to take Mary as my wife. I realize that people will think and say many things about me and Mary. Considering she is with child and we haven't even had our wedding yet, my reputation is going to be stained, as hers will be. This isn't going to be easy.

I would like for it to be easy, but this is the way God has chosen for things to happen—they are part of His plan. Who am I to question His plan? As the prophet

Isaiah said, "God's ways are higher than my ways, and His thoughts higher than mine." The angel told Mary that she would conceive this child by the Holy Spirit, and he confirmed that to me. He also told her that she would be carrying God's Son, and then he confirmed to me that this child would save the people from their sins. She is carrying the Messiah that has been prophesied and we have longed for. Of all the things my people have endured for generations in hope and longing for the Messiah—now He is to come. Having people look at us strangely and talking behind our backs pales in comparison to what others endured as they waited for this day. To be used by God for His purposes is a great honor, and I will commit myself to what He asks of me.

Soon I will go to see Mary and tell her of the dream. I know she will understand my story much better than I did hers yesterday. I'm not sure of what lies before us, but I know God will be with us. This is His plan.

Thoughts to Consider

When God asks us to do something, it can sometimes fly in the face of conventional wisdom. There are assignments that are easy to see and move toward, but there are times when God will ask you to do something in a way that can leave you scratching your head. If it was up to you or me, we wouldn't go about it that way. A key to remember is that when God asks you to do something, He is asking for your obedience not only to do what He has requested, but to do it as He has requested it done. The Bible has several stories where God gave instruction on what to do and how He wanted it done. When man deviated from what and how, there was judgment. When he followed what and how, there was blessing. Commit yourself to doing what God has asked of you the way He has asked you to do it, and expect Him to help you complete it.

Prayer

Father, You know what You are asking of me and how You want me to go about it.

My desire is to be pleasing in Your sight. Show me how You would have me go about what You have asked of me, and help me to stay committed to fulfilling Your will. I trust You to be with me every step of the way. Although I may not have all the answers, I know You do, and that You have gone before me to prepare the way You've asked me to go.

Thank You for Your grace and love in my life and for Your continued faithfulness. I ask this in the name of Your Son, Jesus. Amen.

LITTLE JESUS ASLEEP ON THE HAY

Little Jesus is asleep in Mary's arms, and as I look at them, I can see her eyes are growing heavy as well. We've begun to settle into being parents, and as I think back to everything Mary and I have been through up to this point, it all seems to be an adventure.

We arrived here in Bethlehem after the long journey, and I could see in Mary's face that she was very tired and uncomfortable. Arriving at the time we did, there weren't any rooms readily available with our relatives. Seeing Mary in the condition she was, they quickly led us to a warm, dry area where the animals were often bedded at night. It wasn't the grandest of accommodations by any stretch of the imagination, but the ladies chose it for its privacy and functionality. I had hoped that this night would be so much more for Mary than hay and the scent of livestock.

The arrival of the shepherds and their incredible story of the angelic visitation put things back into perspective. Here amidst the hay and livestock smells, a most holy child was born, and heaven rejoiced to the point of appearing to the shepherds in the countryside to announce the momentous occasion! The Messiah, the Savior of our people, had come into our world in the form of this little babe that Mary has been holding. What an amazing event to behold.

When I think back to the day Mary told me the news of her pregnancy, it was a day I'll never forget. Only hours later I was dreaming and an angel visited me in the dream and confirmed Mary's story, along with giving me instruction on what to do next. Those events were the beginning of my portion of this adventure that we look to be living for the rest of our lives.

I've got to be honest with myself; I have a peace in me that we will be safe and provided for, but I don't have a long-range, detailed plan for the next months or years. I have a good idea of how I would like to see our lives fall into place, but as I've learned over the past months, life doesn't always go as you've planned. As I sit here in Bethlehem with Mary and this little baby, it is so far from what I had envisioned for us. I had been preparing our home in Nazareth when she returned from visiting Elizabeth, and my world was turned upside down.

Through all of the changes to my plans, I must say that God has been faithful to us. When I think of all of the things that we have faced, we have experienced His grace to carry us through time and time again. I don't have a grand understanding of everything we are experiencing now or will face in the future, but I know that I can count on Him to take care of us.

As a builder I like plans, as they help me to construct things. I had a plan for the life Mary and I would build and share, but that plan is just a memory. At first we were too busy for it to bother me much, but as time progressed, there was a part of me that longed for that old plan, that vision of what life was going to be. It has been hard to deal with that sorrow over what might have been, but as I've watched God move in our lives time and time again, I have come to understand that what might have been is not as important as what God wants there to be. My plan was just that—it was MY plan. It revolved around what I wanted. I now understand that God's plan includes me, and I am part of His plan. He has given me Mary as my wife, the woman that He has chosen to be the mother of the Messiah. He has chosen me to be the earthly father of this child, this Holy child. His plan is so much larger than I will ever be able to comprehend, yet He has chosen me to play this part.

I've embraced my part as an honorable part. I am in awe that He chose me, and it makes all the difference in the world to me when I begin to feel inadequate. He wouldn't have chosen me if He did not have plans for me to succeed by His mercy and grace. I am inadequate in myself, but through Him I can do what He has asked of me.

Thoughts to Consider

The plans that we have in life often revolve around ourselves—what we like, what we want, what we think will make us happy, etc. God's plan for us is infinitely larger than the plans we create for ourselves, as His plan involves us in a much bigger plan that belongs to Him. We are selected by Him to play a role in a grand plan He has meticulously thought through and prepared, and He will be there to help us complete our portion if we will look to Him for guidance as we walk out our part.

Prayer

Father, thank You for including me in Your plan and for the plan You have for my life. I ask You to help me to understand what You have created me for and asked of me for my life. I know that You are a good manager, and what You ask of me You prepare me for and provide what I need in order for me to accomplish it. Help me to see Your vision of my life and to walk close to You so that I may fulfill it. Thank You for meeting my every need and Your faithfulness in helping me finish the course You have set before me. I ask this in the name of Your precious Son, Jesus. Amen.

PATIENCE IN SEEING GOD'S WORDS
COME TO PASS

I'm still in awe of the day's events. It seems that sometimes we hear things and realize they are important and special, but slip from in front of our thoughts after the passage of time. I have a tendency to get wrapped up in the daily flow of life, and the details of what in reality were momentous events get lost. Mary does a better job of taking these types of things and holding them near and dear to herself.

Those months ago when the angel appeared to me in my dream and told me of the events that would unfold, I understood the significance of the child Mary was carrying and the role we were both to play. The weeks that followed had us handling a great upheaval of our lives and plans, and for my part I threw myself into preparing our home and life we would be sharing. When the census call came due, we made our trip to Bethlehem, and I knew Mary was due to give birth at any time. That was no excuse that would be accepted by the authorities, so we did what had to be done.

In Bethlehem the child was born, and Jesus came into our lives and world. The events surrounding the birth were less than royal, as she gave birth to Him in a place normally used to shelter livestock, and the little boy slept either on her chest or in the feed trough. We knew it was a special time, even in those conditions, but when the shepherds from outside the city came to find us and tell us of the angel's visitation and tidings to them, it made that night take on a whole new dimension. There in our meager accommodations we saw that God was indeed working His plan in our midst.

So today we found ourselves going to the temple to fulfill the requirements for Mary's purification and Jesus' redemption. We have little in the way of monies but were able to provide the birds as is prescribed by the Law.

We were just another couple coming into the temple with our baby, there to fulfill the Law's requirements. As we walked there, an older man came right up to us, with as bright a countenance as I've seen in many years. He introduced himself as Simeon, commented on the child and on how precious he was, and then asked if he could hold him. Mary handed Jesus to him. It was so interesting to watch him take the babe in his arms, as I could see his excitement but also the care and tenderness he took as he held Him. He gazed into the child's face and then a great look of contentment came across his face. It was as if he felt at total peace. Then he said the following:

> "Lord, now You are letting Your servant depart in peace,
> According to Your word;
> For my eyes have seen Your salvation
> Which You have prepared before the face of all peoples,
> A light to bring revelation to the Gentiles,
> And the glory of Your people Israel" (Luke 2:29-32).

Mary and I stood there stunned. What we knew of the child we had not spoken of openly, yet this Simeon saw little Jesus and spoke even more of Him than what we knew. As we were trying to process his words, he then looked at us and spoke a blessing over us as well, and then spoke to Mary that the child was destined for the rise and fall of many in Israel, and that a sword would pierce her soul. I'm not sure what all of that was about. Mary wasn't sure either, but we think Simeon must have been prophesying of something. After these things he handed the baby back to Mary and went his way.

It was such an odd occurrence, but it made me reflect on those things that have been spoken to Mary and me by the angels over the past months. We really don't have a great understanding of what all is involved with Jesus, but we do understand that He is the Messiah. We have been entrusted with His care.

Here was this man, Simeon, who had been waiting for this day to come, the day when he would see God's Salvation in the flesh. He had been holding onto this promise for years and had kept it in the forefront of his thoughts. When we walked into the temple, he recognized the child as the One he had been waiting for. It made me wonder if I were in his place, with my being so wrapped up in everything I see that needs to be done, would I have been able to see the answer to my promise if it walked past me?

God has been so very faithful to Mary and me in this whole adventure we have been called to. It's a solemn, holy calling

WHEN GOD CHOSE A FATHER

but an adventure in that we have had many twists and turns in it already. The two things I have taken away from today are:

- The majesty and holiness of God's plan for this child, so much that people who have been patiently awaiting God's promise, are brought to tears to see it before their eyes.

- That I need to remind myself of what God has said to me through His angels and His prophets, because those things have not faded away merely because I have not remembered them.

This man Simeon was sustained by the promises he held to. That look on his face as he took Jesus into his arms was priceless. Would that one day I could have that look of contentment, because I know it came from the deepest part of Simeon's being.

Thoughts to Consider

Those things that God speaks to you and me aren't mere words sent to comfort or fill a silent void. They are spoken with an intent for them to come to pass. The passage of time doesn't see God's promises drained of their power. When God says something, He does so expecting it to happen. The question for you and me is, do we expect it to happen as well? There's an old saying that goes, "You can take that to the bank!" Why can it be taken to the bank? Because it is so valid that even the bank will honor it. The bank will take that piece of paper, or statement, and give you money for it because it has value. It's the same way with God's words. They have a recognized value. Do you recognize their value and hold onto them as such? The story of Simeon serves as an encouragement to do so.

Father, thank You for the Bible, Your written words to me, and for the words that You have also spoken to my heart. Help me to value them and expect them to come to pass just as You do. Help me to remain patient as I wait for Your timing for things to come to pass, and to always remember that You are faithful to keep Your Word, regardless of what circumstances may look like. I ask this in the name of Your Son, Jesus. Amen.

The Magi's Visit

What an interesting event took place today!

A group from the East entered Bethlehem today, a caravan like those I have seen traveling near Nazareth on the way of the Sea. To my amazement, they had come to Bethlehem after a long journey specifically to find little Jesus. These Magi had been following a star in the sky that they believed announced the birth of the "King of the Jews" and had travelled a great distance to come and honor Him.

When they first arrived and saw the child, they fell down and worshipped Him.

This wasn't just a group of dignitaries coming to honor a leader; these men had an understanding of how special little Jesus is. It was a precious time for us all.

After they had honored Him with their words, these same men then brought in gifts—gifts that Mary and I were in awe of. As the chests opened, they presented little Jesus gifts befitting a king—gold, frankincense, and myrrh. While I know those items possess more significance than I realize, they were given by the Magi with a very sincere and thoughtful attitude. They had made it their lives' mission to honor this special King.

They visited us for a time, and then excused themselves as they took leave to begin their long journey home. They left with joy on their faces and satisfaction in their hearts, such a long journey to complete a quest that they held as very precious. I have great respect for their dedication.

Thoughts to Consider

Many times the difference between success and failure is the willingness to stick to something to see it through to completion. Endurance is what allows the runner to run a marathon. His steps may not be as fast as other runners, and he may not cover ground as quickly. Through the race he understands that his goal is a destination that will require him to push on when he becomes thirsty, sore, and tired. He understands that his race will not be evaluated for style points along the way, but for crossing the finish line. What have you been asked to complete? What race are you running? Keep the finish line as your goal, and push on until you cross it.

Prayer

Father, help me to keep what You have said is the finish line as my goal and to not be distracted in other directions on my way to finishing my race. Grant me the strength and endurance to overcome any obstacle the enemy may put in my way as I push on to do what You have asked of me. I ask this in the name of Your Son, Jesus. Amen.

FLEEING TO EGYPT

Looking across the sands toward Egypt, I knew that the words of the angel were true, just as they had been in the past. Swiftly uprooting Mary and young Jesus and whisking them away to a foreign land didn't seem like a very practical thing to do, yet Mary and I both had no hesitation to follow the angel's instructions. The Lord had been true to His Word so many times in the past, and we would not question His Word now. Now that I was entrusted with watching over His own Son, I had experienced things that I had only read of before. The gravity of that trust He had bestowed on me seemed at once to be a great blessing and a great weight. While I could do all that was in my might to protect and nurture the child, I was well aware of my own frailty and weakness. It would be by God's hand alone that the child could be properly cared for.

Mary and I have come to understand that only through God's help and guidance could we adequately care for Jesus, and we have become dependent on God to do so. We are so thankful that when He gave us this blessed responsibility, He did not leave us on our own but instead is with us.

When the angel appeared and spoke of the danger to Jesus and the need to make haste and leave our country, Mary and I knew that we must be obedient immediately.

There was an urgency to the angel's directions. The blessing and protection of the Almighty had been announced to us, and it was for us to heed that warning and trust Him once again.

Although she wasn't exactly pleased with the news, Mary hadn't complained and went about preparing to leave. She amazed me with the way she could keep so many things in order while still attending to the child in such a loving and tender manner. Little slipped past her, and next to nothing involving Jesus ever did. She truly loves the child as her own—not out of a sense of duty or an act of obedience. Jesus is her little boy, and even with all the majesty and splendor surrounding His true identity, she still has that look in her eyes when she holds Him—that look of a girl holding her dream close so as not to let it disappear.

I often find her playing with Him, kissing on Him, and telling Him how much she loves Him and how special He is. That special she talks of is how special He is to her. His purpose as foretold by the prophets non-withstanding, He is special to her. She truly loves Him with a mother's love.

It was with that mother's love that she had packed what was needed and scooped Him up as we headed away from the city. In the moments after the angel had given the instruction to leave, I had been thinking of the many different items that needed to be taken care of, checking each off as it was accomplished. My mind had quickly gone to the question, "How will we afford to take this trip and live in a foreign land?"

Almost as quickly as the question had arisen, I remembered the many gifts that the Magi had brought to honor Jesus, and how those rich gifts were more than enough to provide for us on our journey and in setting up a home in Egypt. The Lord had already looked ahead and made provision for us, just as He had for Father Abraham on Mount Moriah. He is so faithful!

Thoughts to Consider

The duties and responsibilities that God gives us are ones that require a response from us. How we respond goes beyond a simple "yes" or "no." How we apply ourselves to the assignment given to us has a major impact on our attitude, our diligence, and our success. Mary and Joseph poured themselves into what had been asked of them regarding being the parents of Jesus. They loved Him and cared for Him as if He were their own. They went beyond just being responsible for Him, as they approached their place in His life as a part of their lives. What has God asked you to do? Are you willing to make it a part of you and not just a duty on a checklist?

Prayer

Father, help me to respond to what You ask of me with my heart, not merely my words. Let my heart and mind be engaged in being all I can be for You as I go about what You have asked of me. As I apply myself to my assignment, show me how I can best accomplish what You have asked of me. I ask this in the name of Your Son, Jesus. Amen.

AWAY FROM HOME AND FAMILY

We've been here in Egypt for several months now and have established a small home for ourselves. The gifts from the Magi were an enormous relief to us as we had to flee so quickly from Bethlehem. We would have had little money and few provisions when we left through the city gate that night to make the long trek into Egypt. I've watched God do many miraculous things in our lives over the past two years.

When we arrived in Egypt, we were able to find a small place where we could reside. I had been concerned about leaving Mary and Jesus alone while I went to look for work. The gold allowed us to afford to become settled in our surroundings before I began leaving them to search for work. It was another example of God knowing what was in our future and making provision for us ahead of time. He has been so faithful.

We had come to a place where we knew no one, and, as a result, no one knew us. In that respect it was good, for no one had any idea of what we had fled from or the identity of Jesus. Even if word of Herod's search for the child did make its way to Egypt, we were just another couple with a small child.

When it was time, I was able to find work rather quickly, as God gave me favor with the local builders. This allowed us to fit into our surroundings and community. While we have made some acquaintances among other Jews in the community, we have found ourselves to be somewhat isolated. Living in a new place in a foreign land has been a trying time for us in that respect.

Mary misses her mother and father a great deal, and I have to be honest and admit that I miss my parents as well. There are many things that we both deal with that we would have liked to have been able to talk to our parents about. Their support for us would be a great comfort. Mary also desires to speak with Elizabeth, as they share a special bond from the events of each conceiving and giving birth to their special children.

I do what I can for Mary, but I am not a woman, I don't think like a woman, and I can't relate to the things women deal with.

We both know we will one day go back to our homeland, but the timing of that return is not known to us. It will be as God wills and instructs. He has kept us safe thus far and will continue to. In the meantime we are doing our best to cope with being away.

We have learned to rely on each other for comfort in a way that I didn't understand earlier. It's an interesting development. I didn't see myself changing in this way, but I have become more aware of and compassionate to Mary when she becomes teary-eyed over these things.

I started out just staring at her, with no idea of how to console her. I would look at her and watch her cry for minutes, fumbling to find a way to try to make things better for her. Over time I learned that she needed to feel secure above all else during those times. I finally understood that she needed to be taken into my arms and held. I had spent weeks trying to think of a way to make things better until I finally realized I couldn't do it on my own.

It was interesting how I fell into this. I asked God to help me find a way to console Mary, and the next time that I came home from work to find her missing home and family, I instinctively took her into my arms and held her. I hadn't tried that before, but it felt like the right thing to do—and it was. She melted into me and sobbed for a bit. Then she looked up with a smile on her face and in her eyes. She nestled her head back on my chest for several more minutes before rising up, her spirit lifted. She was fine the rest of the evening. That evening I learned to quit trying to come up with all the answers for her. Sometimes what she needed was just to know I cared.

We both have also learned to try to focus on what we have together now and not on what we are away from. We can lament the distance between us and our family and friends, but our laments do not shrink the distance or the time away from each other. As Jesus has grown into a walking, talking boy, we've made a conscious decision to change from talking about what everyone is missing to talking about when we see them all soon.

We don't know how soon that "soon" will be, but it has helped us keep focused on that we will see them again, not that we aren't seeing them now. It seems like a small thing, but it has really helped.

There are changes happening in Judea as Herod the Great is in ill health and his sons will probably be succeeding him. As the Romans appoint them over different portions of our precious Israel, possibly the opportunity to return will develop for us. I have come to understand that God's timing is for maximum effect, so I will guard my heart and wait patiently for that time.

Thoughts to Consider

It can be easy to look at your situation, see what isn't going as you would like, and become fixated on those points. Doing this won't change your situation, but it will lead you down a path where you see things through the lens of negativity and disappointment. When you allow this to happen, you fail to see what you have to look forward to because you are fixated on what you believe you are missing. Make the decision to look for the good in where you are and to seek God for His plan for where He is taking you. If you only see the thorns on the rose bush, you will miss the beautiful flowers that adorn it.

~ Prayer ~

Father, thank You for being with me no matter what my situation looks like. Help me to see the positive while I am in the middle of it and to be attentive to Your plan and purpose for me at this time. I thank You that Your thoughts and plans for me are ones that are for hope and a future—good and not evil. Help me to be patient as You work these things out in my life and to show me my part to play as I walk them out. I ask this in the name of Your Son, Jesus. Amen.

RETURNING FROM EGYPT
AND MOVING TO NAZARETH

The journey back to Judea from Egypt was long, but we were able to join a group of fellow travelers and made good time. While I trust in God to watch over us, I know that I must act responsibly as well. We came upon a group of people heading our direction at the same time we needed to depart. Their companionship and the protection we had in numbers were very welcome. We've watched so many things fall into place over the past two years. I can see God's providence over and over.

Arriving back in Judea, I had planned to return to Bethlehem where Mary and I could make a home for our family. The relatives I have there would be welcoming and a big help to us as well. I'm sure that many of the people there would be accepting of us.

As we arrived back in Judea, I understood that Herod's son Archelaus is now in power. Herod's being gone is such a huge relief, as his constant paranoia and violent behavior took life indiscriminately, even that of his own family. My hope in peace after Herod's passing and plans to settle in Bethlehem had been changed. Archelaus has followed in his father's violent ways. We've received word that he had 3,000 people massacred in a single night!

I had another dream—one I know is from God—and I am not to proceed with my plans for settling in Bethlehem. I'm to turn aside and take my family to Nazareth.

Nazareth. I must admit that Nazareth is not exactly the perfect destination for me. We left Nazareth subject to gossip. Mary and I understood to an extent what the reaction to her pregnancy and our marriage would be, but the constant stares and whispering were hard to deal with day after day. Now we are to head back there and make the place our home. We have family and friends there, so we will have support. Coming back will allow us to reunite with them and let them get to know little Jesus.

I should be able to find work in Nazareth or possibly in the ongoing construction in nearby Sepphoris. God will provide; I have watched Him do so many times before, and He will do so again.

When Mary and I first started this path that we were chosen for, we faced so many hardships that were of a personal nature. We understood that following God's instruction and path did not guarantee a life of ease. What it does assure us of is that He will be with us and will bring us through. Moving to Nazareth will be no different. Gossip, stares— they will all fade over time. God's faithfulness will not.

Thoughts to Consider

The twists and turns of life can sometimes lead us in a direction we'd prefer not to go. The Bible contains many stories of people who walked in a relationship with God who saw their life's path take them to places they didn't desire. It was their relationship with God that sustained them during their time in those places and that took them out of those places. When things don't work out as we would like, it can be easy to complain to God, even blame Him for our unhappiness. It's important to remember this truth in life: God is not the cause of our problem; He is our answer to it. He is constantly at work in our lives, but with an understanding of the bigger picture and what impact we can have in it as we are faithful to do as He has asked us.

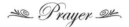

Prayer

Father, there are times when where I am and where I appear to be headed aren't what I prefer. I don't see the big picture as You do, and my perspective has me unsure and uncomfortable about things. Help me understand what I need to know and grant me peace in this time. Calm my fears and give me rest as I trust in You. I don't have the answers here, but I know You do. Thank You for always having my best interests in mind and for Your grace in my life for this situation. I ask this in the name of Your Son, Jesus. Amen.

SEPPHORIS

As the head of the home, it is my duty to provide for my wife and my children. Looking around the village of Nazareth would cause one to believe that a life of farming and raising livestock would be the life each man would lead, but as I look off into the distance toward Sepphoris, I realize that God has given me many opportunities to provide for Mary and the children. The rebuilding of Sepphoris into a city of influence continues, and my skills as an artisan and builder are in demand. While living in Nazareth provides Mary and me with a traditional setting to raise our children, Sepphoris provides an atmosphere of things outside of Israel.

Mary and I cherish the stable environment Nazareth provides, as we who live there are able to raise our families according to the laws and traditions of our forefathers.

We are able to worship and serve the Lord God and to instruct our children in His ways. Nazareth provides us with family and community ties that strengthen us and give us support. Our time away from there while we were in Egypt helped us to better appreciate the simple yet precious things that we had in Nazareth. We have learned to respect and treasure the environment the Lord God has provided for us.

Looking in the direction of Sepphoris reminds me that He has also provided such great opportunity for us, with a growing city within a two-hour walk from our home. As I walk into Sepphoris each day to work on my next project, I see the hand of God at work in our lives. I can still see the Magi visiting us as if it were yesterday. They came to pay homage to Jesus, whom they rightly recognized as a King. The gifts they brought had much significance, as they represented respect, recognition, and homage to the Son of God. I can remember looking at the gold, the frankincense, and the myrrh they had brought and marveling at the amount brought to offer at the feet of our small boy. Only later did I realize that those same gifts would provide for our needs as we traveled and lived in the land of Egypt. Those gifts of honor lived on in our lives to provide for us as the foresight and providence of the Lord God met our every need. He protected us from the hand of Herod, provided for us by using the hands of the Magi, and guided us according to His plan and His timing.

Now He has done the same in this day as my skills are badly needed in a city near to my home. The abilities He has blessed me with and developed in me have brought me favor with those building in Sepphoris, and His hand has brought me to areas that need me and compensate me. As the city continues to be rebuilt and made grander than before, I am able to maintain steady, profitable work. Mary and the children have what they need, and we are able to give out of what we have to others.

Sepphoris also provides us with a bridge to the world outside Nazareth, outside Galilee. While there is much in the city that disgusts me, there is also much that is important that we learn and understand. In the days of our forefathers, Israel had been a kingdom of its own, but the occupations and exiles that followed have left that kingdom as we know it in ruins. Here in Galilee we know firsthand of the Macedonians and their army that conquered and took control of the land, of the Greeks who came and brought their lives, their language, and their gods with them. Later the Romans came into power, and they now occupy and oversee our peoples and lands through the proxy rulers they have placed into positions of authority.

Yes, there is much that these different peoples have brought into my homeland that I disdain, but I also understand that the world they rule is the world I have to live in and that it is important to learn of their language, laws, and ways of doing things. It is important that I and my sons learn how to be Hebrew, serve God, and function in this world. Sepphoris serves this purpose as the young men can learn the language to speak and converse in Greek so that they may be prepared to deal with the Greeks and Romans. There is much learning to be obtained in Sepphoris and opportunity that comes from that learning. Mary and I are careful about what the children will be exposed to, but we do realize that there are things in the city that can benefit them.

Not for a day can I forget that each child is a gift from God that is entrusted to us to love and train up in preparation for serving the Lord God. With Jesus it is even more pronounced, as I know I must do all I can to provide balanced instruction and exposure for Him. Before I know it, He will become a man, and I want to be able to answer to God that I did all I could to prepare Him for manhood and His eventual destiny.

Thoughts to Consider

Each of us is blessed with abilities that God has given us. These can be used in our lives to provide for ourselves and our families. The many responsibilities we each have can keep us so busy that we become wrapped up in our own little worlds, interacting with the world around us but not actually engaging it. It's important that we remember that each of us has a God-given purpose here in the earth, and that the skills we have provide us an avenue and platform that can allow us to learn about our surroundings and in doing so give us insight into how to impact them for God. As we seek God's purpose for our lives, we will discover how we can make a difference in the lives of those around us and be a reflection of God's love to them in the process.

Father, thank You for the abilities and skills with which You have blessed me. Help me to grow in them so that I can be the blessing to others that You have created me to be, and show me how I can use them to be an honorable example of Your love to those come into contact with. I ask this in the name of Your Son, Jesus. Amen.

PREJUDICE IN NAZARETH

I'm not altogether sure what just happened, but I don't really like how things seem since we've come back to Nazareth. Being here while Mary was pregnant with Jesus was hard. The stares, the whispers, they were especially hard on Mary. Pregnant while betrothed. That was a scandal in itself, but then once we completed our marriage ceremony, I watched any deniability I might have chosen to have disappear. It's not that I was going to do so, but the reality hit me that day that I would forever in some people's eyes be the man who couldn't control himself.

The Gentiles would explain away the situation as a lapse of judgment in a moment of passion, but we Jews do not regard it as such. The laws of God and the ways of my people are against the behavior that so many people think we have partaken in. I suppose that was what the incident today was about.

Taking little Jesus out for a walk today to get some fresh air was what Mary and I had set out to do. As we turned the corner and walked into that small group of people, it was quickly apparent that we weren't welcome. The shock on their faces as we rounded the corner and ended up among them is still on my mind. It was a reaction that ranged between recoil and panic. I think the best way I can describe it is like as though walking into a spider's web. There's that initial shock and realization that you've walked into something and then the need to get out of it as quickly as possible.

I thought that I had gotten past letting these types of things bother me, but today it was particularly hard. It's been six months to the day since we came back to Nazareth from our time in Egypt, and I had hoped that we would have settled in and our relationships would have smoothed over after the passage of time. In many cases they have, but it's evident that there are still some who look upon us with prejudice or judgment. Granted, how Mary and I entered into our marriage and starting a family was outside the bounds of what would be considered acceptable. I understand that. I guess I had hoped that people would be able to see past those perceived mistakes and indiscretion and come to accept us. I'm finding that's not always the case.

One thing it is showing me is that I need to be more compassionate to others who have made mistakes. I'm now seeing things from their side—how they are often treated and how it makes them feel. There is no question that we should obey the law and judge rightly according to it. I now find myself thinking upon times that I have looked at others and have gone beyond the law and applied my own feelings and preferences. As I think on this, I find myself wondering how many times I have acted like that group we walked into today and what I can do to be a better person in relation to how I interact with the people I am around.

Here in Nazareth that can be a challenge, but the larger challenge is in Sepphoris, among the Gentiles—especially the Romans. I've found myself looking at the soldiers at times, wondering if they have any regard for the people over whom they enforce Rome's rule. I have to remember that each is someone's son—just as little Jesus is my son to care for and watch over. Many of them may have children of their own. I'd like to believe that they love their children. Seeing them as the arm of Rome is one aspect of who they are, but they are also men who in some ways are like myself. I don't really like the sound of that, but they are. I've even heard that some of the soldiers and even the centurions who lead them have been kind to my people and in cases have given to support the local synagogues or even have gone as far as to become proselytes to our faith.

It's with this in mind that I remember what is most important—to love God and honor Him with both my thoughts and my actions. To honor Him with my thoughts is going to require me to think well of others even when I may not personally like them or appreciate what they have done. I'd want the same done for me. I want the same done for Mary and me now. What I do know is I can't control what others think, but I can work on controlling what I think of others.

Thoughts to Consider

Prejudices come in many forms. They all have their roots in thinking more highly of yourself than someone else. It could be in regards to social status, culture, financial situations, etc. It could be even as petty as not caring for how a person talks or dresses. None of us want to be thought of or treated as less because of these things, but we can inadvertently pass this same judgment on others giving little thought to how we came to these conclusions. Something to remember when you find yourself struggling with this situation is that Jesus died a painful, bloody death on a wooden cross for that person. He placed a great value on them—to the point of giving His life for them. If He saw them as valuable, we should as well. We may not agree with their views, how they dress, etc., but we can look at them as valuable and treat them as such when we interact with them. We should treat others as we want to be treated. It all starts in how we think of them.

 *Prayer*

Father, help me to see others as You see them. Help me to understand that while I may not agree with them, they are still precious in Your sight, and show me how I can love them and show them Your love for them in how I interact with them. Help me guard my heart and my mind so that I will be a source of encouragement to others and not one of hurt or discouragement. I ask this in the name of Your Son, Jesus. Amen.

Entrusted with a Great Responsibility

I was thinking back to a few years ago when the angel appeared to me in the dream and told me to take Mary as my wife. I was going to be the father to a child that wasn't my own—and this child just happened to be the Messiah, God's own Son in flesh. I was in awe. I felt so inadequate, yet so honored.

There were moments where thoughts came to me of how special and favored Mary was to be chosen by God to be the mother of the Messiah. What an honor! Since I was chosen to raise this child as my own son, I was chosen and favored as well.

Chosen and favored. The reality that Mary and I share is that very few people have any idea of the true nature of little Jesus or our part in His life. To most we aren't chosen or favored. We are a disappointment. We are a couple who has operated outside the morals of our people. We aren't very special to most of the people we know.

That caused me to reflect on things with a different perspective, one that is more about where Mary and I live on a daily basis. While we are so highly honored to have this role in our Messiah's life, there is little tangible honor or acclaim that accompanies our roles at this time. Few will be the moments where our roles will be seen or spoken of. In the years to come my name and role in His life will be for the most part a memory to some, but the details will pass away.

When I was chosen and called, I was in a sense special, but I now see that more than anything I was made responsible. I was entrusted with a huge duty and responsibility. What made me special was that God saw me as someone He would trust with the responsibility of being the earthly father to His Son. He made me feel special in His eyes because He trusted me with something so precious to Himself. Now I go about each day trying to always remember that and to conduct myself with that in mind. I'm not as much special as I am responsible.

Whatever God has asked us to do, we are special because He has entrusted us with what He has asked of us. However, when we place the fact *that He has entrusted us and asked of us above the responsibility of what we have been entrusted with*, we fall into pride and begin to live and walk in error. I pray to God that I do not make that mistake and abide in it.

Thoughts to Consider

Being in authority and having the wisdom to use that authority properly don't always go hand in hand. If you've been employed and in the workplace for very long, there is a good chance that you have come across a boss who had authority in an area but didn't exercise it very judiciously. "Because I'm the Boss" is about the weakest justification that can be used to validate a decision. Having the authority to make a decision doesn't make that decision a good one. We can get into error quickly when our *authority consciousness* overrides our *responsibility consciousness*. When you are in a position where authority has been delegated to you, remember that your authority is directly related to what you will be held responsible for. There are times in the workplace where that doesn't seem to be the case, but it always is in God's eyes. We will each give an accounting to Him one day on how we have conducted ourselves.

Prayer

Father, help me to handle authority wisely that I have been given. Let me be ever aware that in Your eyes a leader is to have a servant's heart, and that properly exercising authority involves handling things as You would have them handled. Help me to be mindful of Your character when I work with others, and show me ways in which I can be an example to them of that character. I am under Your authority, and I ask for Your grace to serve You faithfully. May You find my conduct pleasing to You. I ask this in the name of Your Son, Jesus. Amen.

HANDLING THE PRESSURES
OF THE DAY

It was a long walk home from Sepphoris today. It's not that the distance grew in length since I made the same walk yesterday. It has to do with how long the walk seemed. I had much on my mind from the just completed workday. It was a very frustrating day, and that is putting it mildly.

We've been working on our current project for several weeks, and over those weeks things have been run in a loose manner. The overseer of the project comes and goes, spending little time at the project site. When he is there, his attention is usually elsewhere, and he seldom checks with us to find out what issues there may be or needs that we may have. As long as the work seems to be getting done, he makes his appearance and then moves on.

I've found several occasions where his attention could have been used in helping with details for that particular day, but the only way to get an answer from him was to chase him down as he passed through the work site. He will stop and address us when we do this, but we find ourselves pulling away from our site duties in order to pursue him and get his attention. I know he is a busy man, but it seems to me that the title of "overseer" would indicate he is actually looking over everything for the project instead of merely looking to see that he can report to his superiors that progress is being made.

196

I suppose part of my frustration is that I wouldn't handle things in this manner if I were the overseer. Then again, I'm not the overseer. While I have a definite opinion on how things should be handled, it's not my opinion that matters to the people who are financing the project. That's been a bit of a hard pill to swallow and deal with. I know that my opinion does matter, as it's important that I do know how I feel about the situation and why. My problem originally developed from this as I allowed myself to let this fester like a boil would. My discontent was heading toward disillusionment until I thought upon what I had been taught in my early years.

I am responsible for my own tasks. In the case of this building project, I've been helping to fashion the wooden frames for the portico construction, as well as being in charge of the construction of all the needed scaffolding. I've done a good job with those responsibilities and have even been recognized for my performance and my crews' performance.

While we've done an efficient job in our work, we've watched other portions of the project run inefficiently—even to the point of workers being injured. A few simple changes could prevent further injuries and even speed up the building work—but no one seems to be paying much attention. I've had to understand that the overseer's decisions on who is to supervise and what methods will be used are his to make. The few opportunities I have been given to make mention to him of the issues I've noticed, I have had to be very measured in my presentation to him, and it was clear to me that while he was willing to hear me, he was not motivated to change his approach or decisions.

So here I am, walking back to my home in Nazareth, frustrated again because we had to dismantle our scaffolding and relocate it because the stonemasons were given instructions to do work in an area where no thought-out planning had been done. "We want the wall to go here" was the directive. The lead stonemason and I had respectfully requested an audience with the overseer before the work started, but he was unavailable and the work "must stay on schedule as I have reported it would."

The problem was that the location where they had said this wall must go was also a location that had a small fissure in the ground directly below where the wall was to be built. We were going to need to fill the fissure and compact the area to insure it was solid before the wall could be built there and expected to stand firm. Sure enough, after the masons had put up several layers in that area, the wall began to shift and would have eventually failed. We had to move everything out to tear out the stone work and fix the ground beneath it.

I must say that days like today make me glad that I have this walk home. It gives me time to process the events of the day and unwind before I get home to Mary and the children. The frustrations of my day I may speak of to Mary later in the evening after the children are in bed. I've taken home these frustrations at times over the years, and I finally came to realize (with some words from Mary mixed in!) that those frustrations are caused by others, not her and the children. When I come home, I am coming to my place of peace, and to help keep it as such I need not bring the stresses of the day home to replay there. Obviously, those stresses haven't disappeared, but they do not need to continue to swirl and affect my family along with me. Those aren't their stresses and frustrations; they are mine.

With that in mind I am working to do my best to leave them packed away when I come to my home. They will still be there later, but my time at home should be with Mary and the children. Instead of taking those frustrations into my home and, I must in shame admit, allow those frustrations to get the best of me, I must take them and hold them in check as I would a robber trying to invade my home. That's really what they amount to, feelings and thoughts that will rob myself and my family of peace, time, and happiness.

So my really long walk home today did serve two purposes for me today: it got me home, and it got me home with my mind and feelings under control. Work frustrations need not be allowed to turn into home frustrations.

Thoughts to Consider

Life can bring pressures to bear on us from several directions at once. The one place that many of us have that we can be ourselves and unwind is at home. The daily pressures can build over time, and while we monitor ourselves during the day to insure we don't have any unsightly outbursts, arriving home we often let that filter down and what comes out is a river of frustration that gets spewed upon people who aren't the cause. The place and people that should be our haven become the dumping ground for negative feelings, words, and actions. When you arrive home and your frustrations are at a simmer or boil, take a moment to cool. Don't take that pressure into your home and let it dissipate over your family. It gives you no real relief and hurts those around you. Worse, it poisons what should be the well of refreshment in your life. Take control of the situation and make the decision to keep the frustrations from work at work or on the drive home, but don't let them cross the threshold into your home.

Father, help me to handle my workplace in a way that is pleasing to You. Show me how I can be the employee You want me to be and give me favor with those I work with. I ask for Your grace today as I face the pressures of life. Help me to treat my family and home as the haven it can be. Let patience be at work in me, that I may handle things in a way that is pleasing to You. In that patience show me those things in myself that need to be changed and give me the understanding of what things are beyond my control, so that I can place them in Your hands and trust You with them. I ask this in the name of Your Son, Jesus. Amen.

A NEW SON IS BORN

Today Mary gave birth to our son, whom we will name James. This child is of my own flesh and blood, a child born of the shared love between Mary and me. As I look down at this little one, I marvel at his tiny fingers and toes. He seems so small, yet he is already such a big part of our lives.

Jesus is so excited about His baby brother. He marvels over him at least as much as Mary and I do, and He is so very inquisitive about everything involving the baby. It blesses me to see Him so involved and happy. Circumstances surrounding Jesus' birth were so much different for all of us, but then again He is the Son of the Most High. I don't expect to have the same happenings coincide with little James' birth as we did with Jesus.

I can remember looking down at Jesus shortly after Mary had given birth to Him. It was such a joyous event, yet disconcerting in its own right. The Messiah had been entrusted to my care months earlier, but He had been in the womb. Now He was nestled in my arms, a small bundle sleeping peacefully— small, helpless, and the hope of all generations at the same time. He was born *for* me, but not *of* me. I understood that it was essential that I was not His physical father, but it was a battle to overcome the thoughts that had assaulted me for months regarding that fact. Yet the grace of God was with me to strengthen me and give me peace in times when despair would seek to have its way. In my reliance on Him I have never been failed.

And now I hold little James, my son who is of me. My line will now pass down through him, a line that traces back to the House of David. He will be another son who will make his mother smile and his father proud.

Looking down at him, I understand how much a gift of God this child is to us. All children are gifts from God entrusted into our care to protect and nurture them until they grow to adulthood, at which time what we have diligently taught them will become that which guides them. Having little Jesus in our lives has taught me the precious gift that each child is. In truth, all children are of God and come from Him. We as parents are stewards of God's children and are accountable for how we handle them.

I know that James will be different from Jesus. I understand that the nature of sin is not in Jesus, but only that of God. Little James has been born into this world with the nature of sin. Then again, all children are unique. We will spend the next years getting to know little James for who he has been created by God to be. I must admit what will be a new challenge for me is learning to parent a child that has been born with a sinful nature! Time spent with our families will serve Mary and me well in the coming years!

How does one take in a child that is not his own and call him his son? How does he love him as his own? How does one love a child that has come from his own body?

How do you balance the two? So many questions for which I have had few answers.

How does one believe his betrothed when she tells him after returning from time away at her cousin's that she is pregnant, and that she has known no man—that she has conceived by the Spirit of God? I can tell you—you don't at first. But as your understanding is increased and things are revealed to you by the providence of God, you learn to do so by faith. Once the angel had spoken to me and revealed the plan and will of God to me regarding the child, I moved on trusting in the words He had spoken. In the same manner, I will approach raising these children as one in the family with whom God has blessed Mary and me. I have come to understand that while I do not have many answers, the providence of the Almighty guides and preserves us. In Him I place my trust and move forward. Just as He has been faithful to provide for us in every situation up to this point, He will do so in the future.

I wonder when James will come to understand the honor that God has bestowed upon him in allowing him to grow up in the same home as the Messiah, to be able to call Him brother. It isn't that our home is anything special of its own, but that the presence of God is in it, both in spirit, and in the flesh in our son Jesus. Yes, I call Him my son, because He is known to everyone as my son. And I do love Him as my own, more than I had believed possible those times ago. Now I have another son—James.

My father had explained that it is possible to love each of his children the same, yet differently. I'm now beginning to understand what he meant. You do not love one child greater than another, but as each child is unique, your love for that particular child is different in relation to them. That love is an appreciation for the unique qualities that make them who God created them to be. It's so very important to let the love you have for someone be based on who they are, and not how they make you feel. I'll have to watch myself in this area, just as my father had advised me. James is of my flesh, so in that I could favor him more than Jesus. Jesus will be much better behaved, and in that I could favor Him more than James. Then there is the issue of Jesus as the Messiah. I will be diligent to follow through, and I know Mary will watch over me to make sure I am balanced. She always does.

Thoughts to Consider

Loving people for who they are isn't always a given. There are some people who are easier to love than others. It can be their personality, their actions, or their talk, but there is something about them that requires us to dig a little deeper within ourselves to respond to them with kindness. It's that digging deeper that is required of us. In God's eyes we don't get a pass on trying to reach out to that person with kindness and respect. We are His ambassadors and are expected to conduct ourselves with that in mind. Sometimes the hardest place to practice this is in the home. Home is the place where we let our guard down and also where we have the most influence and accountability. Learning how to navigate our children—from our own body or another's—is a responsibility that we must not shirk. Take the time to evaluate your feelings and then make adjustments as are needed. You are having a direct influence in each of those lives, and you will be held accountable. Whether you acknowledge it or not, you are directly involved in shaping lives. Ask yourself this sobering question: "If they were to decide the inscription about me on my headstone, would I be proud of what they chose to say?" Treat them in such a way that years from now when they think of your impact on their life, they are thankful for who you chose to be to them.

Prayer

Father, help me to be ever mindful of the honor You have given me to be an influence in people's lives. Give me wisdom on how to relate to those You have placed in my life, and in how I can be to them what they need. I ask You to fill in the spaces in their lives I cannot fill and to be to them what they need in the areas in which I am deficient. I thank You for working in me by Your Holy Spirit to make me a better person and Your faithfulness in helping me be to them all that You want me to be. I ask this in the name of Your Son, Jesus. Amen.

PASSOVER IN JERUSALEM

It was an exciting day in Jerusalem today! Mary and I took Jesus to the temple to witness the sacrifices. He was so wide-eyed at first as the priests began the rituals, but then after a bit we noticed how enthralled He became with watching all the details He could see. Mary and I knew that this day was coming when He would witness these things firsthand. We can't even begin to guess what was going through His mind as He watched the priests offering the sacrifices on the altar. We know the writings of the prophets regarding the Messiah. Jesus is aware of them as well. His command of the scriptures is amazing for a boy His age. Even now we wonder how much of who He is and what lies ahead of Him is He truly aware of. The destiny before Him is beyond our comprehension. Did He recognize the shadow of things to come as they relate to Him?

I did my best to explain every detail of what was going on with the rituals. At times He would finish my sentences. He wasn't being unruly; it was His excitement that brought on His exuberance. I'm in awe of what He knows and understands. We have done our best to teach Him and provide Him with the means to study the scriptures. The teachers in the synagogue have been good with Him as well, although they don't understand who He is and is destined to become. Mary and I hold that closely to ourselves. I watch her with Him, and I know she has insights that I do not. She is a thinker, my Mary. The things that have been spoken over Him through the years she remembers and patiently waits on. I still marvel at how she is with Him and for how He is with her for that matter. There is no doubt that He loves His mother.

I know He loves me as well, but they have that something special between a mother and her son. As He is now close to manhood, He is growing in how He looks to her. He has taken on a new sense of responsibility and care for her, just as a son of His age should do. With Jesus it isn't about duty or tradition. It's in His eyes; He does it for the love He has for her. I know there is so much more in Him than what I have taught and shown Him, but my hope is that how He has seen me love Mary has been a help in Him getting to where He is now. My hope is that the look He has in His eyes for her is the one He sees in my eyes when I look at her and am with her. While my love for her is that of a husband and not a son, there is still much that is in common between the two.

Thoughts to Consider

What are you modeling for your children? Sending them to school to be taught is important. Attending church and being involved there is important. What are they seeing in you on a daily basis that they are incorporating into who they are? How do they see you treat others? More importantly, once they see you interact with others, what do they hear you say afterwards? We are constantly providing an image that our children see and model themselves after. Do you keep that in mind when you are around them? How your son treats other women will be influenced by what he sees you do towards them, even your attitudes. How your daughter hears you talk about their father or other men will have an influence on how she regards fathers, husbands, and men in general. One of the greatest gifts we can give our children is our example. Show them how a mother loves, how a father loves, how a husband and wife love. It's not too late to start, even if you haven't done well in the past. Be honest and let them know you were a poor example back then, but going forward you are going to be a good example. A late gift is still accepted and shows that you care.

Prayer

Father, You have given me the responsibility of being an example to my child of who You want to be to them. Help me to be more like You in all I say or do, so that they may see Your goodness working in me. For the times I've failed in the past, I ask for Your forgiveness and that You strengthen me to live each coming day before You and my child in a way that shows them love, respect, and kindness. Grow them to walk before You in a way that is pleasing to You, and that I may be an example of that walk from this day forward. I ask this in the name of Your Son, Jesus. Amen.

OUR SON ISN'T A CHILD
ANY LONGER

It took us the better part of the day, but we finally found Jesus. Looking back over the past days, I now see where we probably should have been searching for Him among the teachers of the Law first. From a young age He has had a hunger for the scriptures, and His understanding of them is beyond His years. He loves to talk of the Law and of God, as He seeks out any opportunity to study or engage in conversation regarding them. When we arrived at the temple, I saw His excitement and fascination as we watched the priests. He was taking in every sight and every sound. This trip was very special to Him and one He had anticipated for a long time.

When it was time to return to Nazareth, Mary and I hadn't given much thought to His not being with our group as we left. He was almost a man and knew that we would be leaving. He had been with some of the other children His age at other times, and we had assumed He was still with them. When we had seen some of the boys, we thought He was with them. It was quite a surprise to us when we later discovered that He wasn't anywhere to be found with our group. When the boys said they had last seen Him while we were still in Jerusalem, Mary and I became very concerned. We headed back to Jerusalem as quickly as possible and began our search for our son.

My first thought was, "Great! God has entrusted me with His own Son and now I've lost Him!" Many thoughts came during the days we searched for Him, but I chose to remind myself of the different instances of God's faithfulness to us over the years, and how He had protected our family—specifically Jesus. He would protect Him now as well.

We came upon Him in the temple among the teachers. Mary wanted to run directly to Him and take Him in her arms. My first inclination was to be authoritative and demand He answer for His actions, but as I listened to Him discussing the scriptures with the teachers I held back and placed my hand on Mary's shoulder to have her do the same.

It was obvious that they were deep in discussion with Him, and that there was a level of understanding passing between them all that was beyond what a twelve-year-old boy should bring. I looked around those who were watching and listening, and they seemed as astounded as I was. This son of mine was operating in a wisdom and knowledge far beyond anything I possessed, and He was among some of the more respected teachers in Jerusalem.

As soon as there was a pause in the conversation, Mary and I stepped forward to make Jesus aware of our presence and His need to come with us. Mary looked at Him and in her stern mother voice asked Him:

> *"Son, why have You done this to us? Look, Your father and I have sought You anxiously."*

The words that came out of His mouth in response were not defiant or disrespectful. They were matter of fact.

"Why did you seek Me? Did you not know that I must be about My Father's business?"

Mary and I still aren't sure what that was all about. "My Father's business." Staying behind without our knowledge and staying in the temple with the teachers doesn't sound like something that would be considered my business. I'm not qualified to sit among them, and my business isn't conducted in the temple. The temple is a holy place. My business is conducted in my workshop or at the work site.

"Why did you seek Me?"

We thought the more pressing question that needed to be answered was, *"Why did You not leave when we were supposed to and go home as You knew was planned?"* When we asked Him, He was genuinely apologetic for worrying us, but it was obvious He thought He was doing right by staying in the temple. We'll have more conversations about this tonight and in the coming days; that is for sure.

I'm realizing that He is almost a young man now, and our role in His life will change. It is the same progression my father went through with me, and I will go through it with my other sons as well. This is an adjustment I'll have to make, but I'm not sure what all will be involved or how to deal with it on a personal level. I'm sure father can share with me from his own experience. For the rest I'll need to trust in God to help me handle this time in our lives.

Next year when we come for Passover, we will have some definite times and rendezvous points agreed upon to make sure this doesn't happen again. I'm worn out.

Thoughts to Consider

One of the harder things in being a parent is having to adjust on the fly as you find your child getting older and moving into new stages of maturity. It seems that you finally get a working knowledge of a child in a certain age range and then they move on to another maturity level. As they become teenagers and then into their twenties, the landscape makes some drastic changes that a parent has to adjust to. The parenting role shifts from "All Knowing Regent" to "Financier and Parental Unit" to "Trusted Advisor"—and that is if your relationship remains solid! Just as the child is maturing and learning to navigate into adulthood, so is the parent adjusting to the child's adjusting. This is a *natural process*. Don't allow it to become another one of life's cruel tricks on you. Embrace this new place in life you have found yourself in and ask God to help you navigate it. He has the answers to help you not only survive it but to be a blessing to your children in it.

Prayer

Father, I thank You for the beautiful child You have blessed me with. I know that this was Your child first and always will be. Help me to understand my changing role in their life, and how to be the parent they need me to be in this time in their life. Give me peace for this new place where I find myself, and I ask that You give me insight into ways I can best share with them the wisdom and experience that I have. I ask this in the name of Your Son, Jesus. Amen.

Made in the USA
Columbia, SC
22 December 2022

74639561R00129